CONTEMPORARY WRITERS

General Editors
MALCOLM BRADBURY
and
CHRISTOPHER BIGSBY

MARGARET DRABBLE

IN THE SAME SERIES

Donald Barthelme   *M. Couturier and R. Durand*
Saul Bellow   *Malcolm Bradbury*
Richard Brautigan   *Marc Chénetier*
E. L. Doctorow   *Paul Levine*
John Fowles   *Peter Conradi*
Graham Greene   *John Spurling*
Seamus Heaney   *Blake Morrison*
Philip Larkin   *Andrew Motion*
Doris Lessing   *Lorna Sage*
Malcolm Lowry   *Ronald Binns*
Iris Murdoch   *Richard Todd*
Joe Orton   *C. W. E. Bigsby*
Harold Pinter   *G. Almansi and S. Henderson*
Thomas Pynchon   *Tony Tanner*
Alain Robbe-Grillet   *John Fletcher*
Philip Roth   *Hermione Lee*
Kurt Vonnegut   *Jerome Klinkowitz*
Patrick White   *John Colmer*

MARGARET
DRABBLE

JOANNE V. CREIGHTON

METHUEN
LONDON AND NEW YORK

For my parents,
Bernice and William Vanish

First published in 1985 by
Methuen & Co. Ltd
11 New Fetter Lane, London EC4P 4EE
Published in the USA by
Methuen & Co.
in association with Methuen, Inc.
733 Third Avenue, New York, NY 10017

© *1985 Joanne V. Creighton*

Typeset by Rowland Phototypesetting Ltd
Printed in Great Britain by
Richard Clay (The Chaucer Press) Ltd
Bungay, Suffolk

British Library Cataloguing in Publication Data

Creighton, Joanne V.
Margaret Drabble. – (Contemporary writers)
1. Drabble, Margaret – Criticism and interpretation
I. Title
823'.914   PR6054.R25Z/
ISBN 0-416-38390-4

Library of Congress Cataloging in Publication Data

Creighton, Joanne V., 1942–
Margaret Drabble.
(Contemporary writers)
Bibliography: p.
1. Drabble, Margaret, 1939–
– Criticism and interpretation.
I. Title.   II. Series.
PR6054.R25Z63   1985   823'.914   85-2928
ISBN 0-416-38390-4 (pbk.)

CONTENTS

	General editors' preface	6
	Preface and acknowledgments	8
	A note on the texts	11
1	Introduction	13
2	Bird-cages	37
3	Golden realms	65
4	Urban ground	91
	Notes	113
	Bibliography	121

GENERAL EDITORS' PREFACE

The contemporary is a country which we all inhabit, but there is little agreement as to its boundaries or its shape. The serious writer is one of its most sensitive interpreters, but criticism is notoriously cautious in offering a response or making a judgement. Accordingly, this continuing series is an endeavour to look at some of the most important writers of our time, and the questions raised by their work. It is, in effect, an attempt to map the contemporary, to describe its aesthetic and moral topography.

The series came into existence out of two convictions. One was that, despite all the modern pressures on the writer and on literary culture, we live in a major creative time, as vigorous and alive in its distinctive way as any that went before. The other was that, though criticism itself tends to grow more theoretical and apparently indifferent to contemporary creation, there are grounds for a lively aesthetic debate. This series, which includes books written from various standpoints, is meant to provide a forum for that debate. By design, some of those who have contributed are themselves writers, willing to respond to their contemporaries; others are critics who have brought to the discussion of current writing the spirit of contemporary criticism or simply a conviction, forcibly and coherently argued, for the contemporary significance of their subjects. Our aim, as the series develops, is to continue to explore the works of major post-war writers – in fiction, drama and poetry – over an international range, and thereby to illuminate not only those works but also in some degree the artistic, social and moral assumptions on which they rest. Our wish is that, in their very variety of approach and emphasis, these books will stimulate interest in and understanding of the vitality of a living literature which, because it is contemporary, is especially ours.

Norwich, England   MALCOLM BRADBURY
                                       CHRISTOPHER BIGSBY

PREFACE AND ACKNOWLEDGMENTS

To those who have seen her as a rather traditional, middle-brow, popular women's writer, Margaret Drabble could be a surprising inclusion in a series concerned with the changing spirit and character of contemporary fiction. Some of Drabble's own comments have contributed to the impression that she is a hard-line fictional conservative, disdainful of contemporary experiment: "The experimental novel – well, a lot of it seems to be like making films about Buddhist monks. It seems to me very irrelevant." But statements like this were made in the 1960s, early in her career, and they were responses to very specific kinds of radical experiment at that time. Today she readily accepts that the novel must be protean and reflective of its times – and her own fiction has, in fact, always been so. While Drabble's work has demonstrable formal and moral links to traditional realistic fiction, these links are obliquely established through an informing modern consciousness: literate, inquiring, ironic, bemused. It is precisely this mediating and often equivocal position between the traditional and the modern which makes her an important voice in contemporary fiction and links her to other writers of her generation. I use "voice" deliberately, for I believe that her style is characterized by the personal narrative voice – which is often quite different from that of the author behind it. It is, I think, this authenticity of voice which draws readers to her work.

And readers, both general and critical, are drawn to her

work in remarkable numbers. Her American and Canadian audience is extensive and enthusiastic. In fact, her critical reputation is arguably higher in North America than in Great Britain. Widely distributed (and now critically studied) in many other countries – including Japan, India, and Turkey, where Drabble has lectured – her novels are translated into all the major European languages, including French, German, Russian, Dutch, Bulgarian, and Yugoslavian, as well as Japanese. I believe it is important to try to understand the popularity of her work. Why does a writer who is in many ways so rooted and grounded in "Englishness" have such international appeal?

Clearly, Drabble's reputation is in part gender-based. She is perceived as a woman writing credibly about modern women. Even though she has now moved beyond the exclusively women-centered books of her early fiction, and is somewhat "fed up" with being labelled a women's writer, she has seemed to speak directly for and to a whole generation of women. The compelling female voice – or voices – of her work was what drew me, an American, initially to her work. Feminist issues are, Drabble claims, the abiding subject of enquiry on the part of her audiences as she travels about the world on British Council lecture tours. But, important as gender is, it would be wrong to suggest that it is the sole basis of her importance and popularity. The resonances of her work, I will argue here, grow out of her strong sense of the powers and resources of existing literary traditions, coupled with her intelligent portrayal of the familiar problems of people in modern society, and her aware-ness of the moral and formal changes this forces on the contemporary novelist. She mediates between determining contexts, be they "male" or "female" concerns and traditions, literary or popular issues and perspectives, individual or so-cietal needs and obligations, traditional or modern ways of perceiving and writing. Her Forsteresque attempt to "only connect" diverse strains in English life and literature, along with her willingness to accept accommodation, irresolution, and openness to contingency, account for the distinctively

9

"Drabblesque" tone of her fiction, so compelling to some readers, so exasperating to others, a tone which is, above all else, contemporary and serious.

Of the many people who have offered valuable encouragement, advice and assistance I would like to single out for special thanks Malcolm Bradbury, along with Christopher Bigsby, Janice Price, Ellen Cronan Rose, Joan Korenman, David Leon Higdon, and Edward Stanulis. I thank Weidenfeld & Nicolson for permission to quote from Drabble's texts; Bernard Oldsey, editor of *Contemporary Literature*, for permission to reprint a revised portion of an essay entitled "The Reader and Modern and Post-Modern Fiction," 9 (1982); G. K. Hall & Co. for permission to reprint, in a different form, an essay, "Reading Margaret Drabble's *The Waterfall*," which appeared in *Critical Essays on Margaret Drabble*, edited by Ellen Cronan Rose (Boston, 1985); and Wayne State University for a Faculty Research Award and a Sabbatical Leave making possible the research and writing of this study. I am especially grateful to Margaret Drabble herself who graciously and candidly talked with me in September 1979 and June 1984, and who checked the factual accuracy of an earlier draft of the manuscript. I am solely responsible for the views put forth in this book.

Detroit, 1984   JOANNE V. CREIGHTON

A NOTE ON THE TEXTS

Page references to quotations from Margaret Drabble's fiction are taken from the Penguin editions. The following abbreviations have been used:

SBC *A Summer Bird-Cage*
GY *The Garrick Year*
M *The Millstone*
JG *Jerusalem the Golden*
W *The Waterfall*
NE *The Needle's Eye*
RG *The Realms of Gold*
IA *The Ice Age*
MG *The Middle Ground*

1

INTRODUCTION

Margaret Drabble is an ambitious writer with broad social concerns who plays a lively role in both popular and literary culture. Varied and considerable, her writing grows out of a genuine engagement with contemporary issues and an engrained sense of literary historicism. Besides her nine novels to date, she has written several stories and screenplays, a biography of Arnold Bennett and other literary books, and has edited several texts on literary subjects. She has written scores of reviews and other pieces – from short notes to extended essays – for literary and popular journals, newspapers, and magazines. Comfortably attuned to audience, she writes for both school children and adults, both scholars and laymen. She is seemingly equally at home writing about disciplining children or travelling abroad, sexual mores or public policy, current television shows or the Victorian age. Evident throughout her career is her concern with the social problems concomitant with historical change, a concern brought increasingly into the foreground in her more recent, broadly based social realism. Not at all reclusive or personally disengaged, she has appeared on televised literary programs and participated in governmental councils, Arts Council committees, and British Council lecture tours, and for years taught adult education one day a week at Morley College in south London. She has just completed an ambitious five-year project, the re-editing of the *Oxford Companion to English Literature*. Unworried about this disruption of her novelistic career, Margaret Drabble has a disingenuous lack of professional earnestness, an openness to contingency, to the changing phases and opportunities of her life, to the varying contexts in which she lives. She seeks to be an "inquiring mind" rather than a professional bound and labelled, committed and obligated, predictable and steady. This attitude underlies her insistence that she is a writer who writes on literary topics rather than a literary critic. She has chosen deliberately, she says, the freedom of an unaffiliated writer, untied to an academy, an ideology, or a methodology. It is a choice with literary, political, and ethical implications, affecting how and what she writes.

Her critical writing is confident, engaged with the subject, engagingly personal, disarmingly "non-scholarly" in posture: she does not hesitate, for example, to interject personal commentary into her discussions. Her biography of Arnold Bennett, one could argue, is as interesting for what she says about herself as for what she says about him. Her novels, too, are personal in tone – lucid, seemingly confessional, eminently readable. Their protagonists have generally followed the course and concerns of her own life: young women leaving university, getting married and separated, birthing children, having affairs, raising progressively older children, reaching midlife, wondering what next. In fact, one commentator has claimed that Drabble's work might be thought of as an English *Passages* for a particular generation of middle-class women. Now, as her work has broadened, she has been called a central chronicler of contemporary urban middle-class life.

Neither ivory tower artist nor academician, Margaret Drabble seems attuned to herself and to ordinary experience, vividly rendering the ordinary with intelligence and learning, insight and humor. This lack of intellectual pretension has contributed to her accessibility and popularity – and, in some quarters, an underestimation of her qualities. One recurrent view is that she has had an extraordinarily lucky sense of timing rather than talent:

14

Her fame and significance have been treated in a way that is out of proportion both to the quantity and quality of her output. In retrospective assessment of the nineteen-sixties, it may well appear that Margaret Drabble's greatest gift lay in her sense of timing; she was historically fortunate enough to appear on the literary scene as the first English woman to give voice to the delusive promise of college life, followed by the cold douche of matrimony and child-bearing.[1]

It is easy but erroneous to confuse Drabble's lucidity and her focus on the ordinary – particularly ordinary women's lives – with ordinary work. Her attempt to come to terms with women's changing role in modern society is serious, searching and important, as women around the globe have recognized. Fundamentally liberal and humanistic, Margaret Drabble is committed to the idea that novels should be about common human experiences and should be "available to a fairly large reading public, by which I don't mean popular novels, I mean novels that aren't esoteric or hermetically sealed," or exclusively "a clever array of symbolic patterning for the scholarly mind."[2]

Her works are lucidly contemporary, and yet informed with a sophisticated sense of literary history and tradition. Because she attracts, like few writers can, both general readers and literary critics, her work draws together middlebrow and serious fiction, helping to resynthesize a readership split by modernist élitism. Actively participating both in ordinary, middle-class British life and in intellectual and literary circles, she is one of those seminal writers who writes out of deep engagement with the culture in which she lives. Assimilating, creating, pronouncing judgment upon literary form and value, she also gives voice to common problems, to communal concerns. The danger in playing this role too strenuously is that she will see herself and be seen as a public personage with opinions to peddle. Aware of these dangers, she claims she is tired of appearing on television panels and of voicing in a variety of settings her opinion on a wide range of political, social, and literary questions. Similarly, her fiction is most successful when it is questioning, equivocal, open to possibility rather than rhetorical or committed to a particular view. She has also been accused of being too responsive to what's happening around her, of being, in other words, a little too up-to-date, trendy, and glib, rather than intellectually serious. This, in some senses, seems to me patently untrue. In spite of her disarming disingenuousness, Margaret Drabble is undeniably an erudite and serious person, deeply – even stolidly – based in tradition, genuinely engaged with her subject matter. It is true, however, that she is not a philosophical writer – a Saul Bellow or a George Eliot – capable of memorably and profoundly articulating the human issues implicit in her work, even though she admires and strives to emulate these writers. She has yet to find the right voice for the omnisciently narrated, broadly based social realism she is determined to write these days, a direction that I think may not be the most productive path for her. Her real strength as a writer – and her popularity – have grown out of the more modest scope of her earlier fiction: the psychological resonance, the vivid particularization and credible voices of her characters, the acute observation of the details of ordinary life.

*

Frequently interviewed and photographed, the subject of several feature articles, including an hour-long BBC documentary "One Pair of Eyes," Margaret Drabble is more personally knowable than more reclusive writers. She told me she is both "very diffident and very gregarious," a combination borne out in her interviews and conversation, which are often a curious blend of disclosure and circumspection. Looking back now after the recent deaths of her father in 1982 and her mother in 1984, she is thoughtful and candid about the childhood and family background which have had such a determining effect upon her fiction.[3]

Born on 5 June 1939, in Sheffield, Yorkshire, she is the daughter of John Frederick and Marie Bloor Drabble. Her father was a barrister, then a circuit judge for Suffolk and Essex, and later, in retirement, a novelist. Her mother was an English teacher at The Mount in York, a Quaker school her daughters were later to attend. The first in their families to go to university, both parents graduated from Cambridge. While Drabble has characterized her rearing as "very tolerant, liberal, middle class, professional," she none the less feels close to her working-class roots, and is especially conscious of her mother's difficult transition into the middle class. Her father worked in his family's business, a small sweet factory, to save money before reading law at Cambridge. Her mother's family were potters from the Potteries in Staffordshire. Indeed, Drabble comments in her biography of Bennett:

> His childhood and origins . . . are very similar to my own. My mother's family came from the Potteries, and the Bennett novels seem to me to portray a way of life that still existed when I was a child, and indeed persists in certain areas. My own attitudes to life and work were coloured by many of the same beliefs and rituals, though they were further in the past for me, but as Bennett knew all too well they were attitudes that die hard. He might have been surprised to find how closely I identify with them, after two or three generations of startling change. (*Arnold Bennett*, p. xii)

In particular she isolates Bennett's resentment of the "joyless-ness of life in provincial towns," his "disdain for conventional Sunday school religion," and his "need to escape" which was felt throughout her family, particularly by her mother.

One of the most graphic depictions of this need for escape from provincial limitations is *Jerusalem the Golden* (1967), set in Northam, a fictionalized Sheffield, a novel which Drabble readily acknowledges in her biography was "profoundly affected" by Bennett's attitudes as well as her own background: "I can't quite distinguish what came from where" (p. 48). Clara Maugham's "escape" from the North is problematic, as is Simon Camish's in *The Needle's Eye* (1972), Frances Wingate's in *The Realms of Gold* (1975) – and

Margaret Drabble's. Her northern origins, she admits, are an indelible part of her being. More than many writers she believes in the profound "effect of landscape upon the soul." In fact, she has written a literary topology, *A Writer's Britain* (1979), an eloquent testimony to her belief in the paramount importance of place in shaping both character and literature. In her own fiction houses and landscapes become metaphors of the body and of the self. Houses are intimately expressive of their inhabitants; landscapes can be read as "electrocardiograms of childhood." Her characters are rooted and circumscribed within a particular mind and body, house and geography, family and history, language and culture, time and place. *The Realms of Gold*, for example, is a study of a family encumbered with what is called the "midland sickness," and it records Frances Wingate's rediscovery of her northern past and the re-rooting of her identity in a sense of family and place.

Equally important in Drabble's work is social class; she portrays with poignancy and credibility the debilitating effects of class consciousness on middle-class aspiration – a particularly vivid example of this is Simon Camish in *The Needle's Eye*. Her novels expose the emptiness, the waste, the aimlessness of middle-class lives. Her later works are a powerful criticism of the spiritual paucity of contemporary materialistic goals, and the lack of connection between humanistic values and changing ordinary life. Deeply influenced as a young girl by *Pilgrim's Progress*, Drabble creates characters, like Bunyan's, who are wending their way through an uncharted "moral landscape," a world where old values are no longer tacitly accepted and new views are unclear. Knowing only too well that they have been shaped and maimed by forces larger than the self, they question whether they can impose a shape upon their lives at all. "There's nothing I can do about my nature, is there?" asks Rosamund at the end of *The Millstone* (1965, p. 144), hoping she's wrong, hoping psychological determinism had not "got its claws" into her to the extent that Simon Camish of *The Needle's Eye* depressingly fears it has into him. While insistently moral in focus, her work both demonstrates the difficulty of applying moral standards to the multifarious situations of modern life and examines the deterministic effects of geography, social class, family, economic status, politics, religious training and the decidedly English context of her characters' lives.

Her own religious views were shaped by her parents' liberal attitudes and her Quaker schooling at The Mount in York. The Drabbles were not Quakers at the time – Mr Drabble took the children to the Anglican church; Mrs Drabble was an atheist – but they were sympathetic to Quaker values and in later years joined the Society of Friends. Margaret Drabble was infused both at boarding school and at home with the belief that God "was in every man, making him equal and worthy of respect." She recalls that as children they would discuss and puzzle over the implications of this concept. Was there the light of God in Hitler? In Genghis Khan? They were also taught to live their lives not to their own satisfaction, but in contribution to the general good. She says that the Quakers are "more liberal in their social values than the conventional girls' public school. They don't have rules. They believe in moral pressure, not punishment," and adds that "the moral pressures from my parents were probably very strong, too."[4]

The belief taught at Margaret Drabble's Quaker school in a "light of God" in everyone, in the efficacy of good works, is undercut in Drabble's thinking by a residue of Calvinistic belief in a deterministic universe where some are blessed and others damned. Such a world is intolerable, especially if one is forced to conclude, as she herself must, that one is of the elect: "fate has really given me a wonderful deal, a magnificent hand of cards. . . . I'm really egalitarian at heart. I think everyone should have the same hand of cards when they're born."[5] One of the most recurrent themes in her work and commentary is her puzzlement over the interrelationship of free will and determinism: "Fate and character are irreconcilable. That's why I write the books. The whole point of writing a novel, for me, is to try to work out the balance between these two, and there is no answer."[6] While not doctrinally religious, she readily acknowledges belief in something larger than the finite, the individual, and the material: "I don't believe that this material world is all. I can't bring myself to think that there's even a sensible way of looking at things."[7] And certainly she subscribes to a religious consciousness, an ethical commitment to play a responsible part in the human community. Her participation – in addition to her writing – consists largely of her active committee work for various progressive causes. She is moved occasionally, but reluctantly, to political activism such as her participation in a demonstration at the Foreign Office (1971) against the Rhodesian settlement and, more recently, the World Disarmament Campaign protest (June 1981) outside the House of Commons.

"One's relationships with one's siblings and parents is something that you're going to write about again and again, in different forms," admits Margaret Drabble.[8] A central generating tension in many of her novels resides in mother–daughter (and, in *The Needle's Eye*, mother–son) relationships. Father figures, in contrast, are shadowy and comparatively unimportant. She has said that her own father was away for the war, very busy during periods of her childhood, and rather "remote," although she also points out that he was loving and supportive. Her relationship with her mother was, obviously, more intense and more complicated. Mrs Drabble recalls in an interview for *People* magazine (13 October 1980) that Maggie "was a fiery child with a hyperactive mind. She gave me many sleepless nights." Maggie remembers particularly and painfully her mother's neurotic insecurity and depression – rooted in "class reasons" – which cast an inhibiting cloud over the family's home life and social interaction. While her father made a "perfect transition to the middle-class barrister life; he spoke very good English; he had a very good presence and a very social manner; he was very easy and affable and people thought him charming," her mother "continued to speak broad Yorkshire and was the reverse of charming: she was aggressive, rude, difficult, shy, all in one, and that meant that their social life was terribly difficult. . . . And I think there is more of that in English life than one would believe possible, more scars from social encounters." It seemed to Margaret as a small child that "the home was a place to wither away in; there was no way you could have friends, and that made me very, very insecure. I mean, as a child I had a most terrible stammer. I could hardly speak."[9] She claims only to have been happy when away at boarding school. Appreciating the struggles her mother underwent to overcome social, economic and gender barriers – "My mother ground her teeth and everybody said, 'How unattractive' – and I was in a position because of circumstances of education and money to be able to profit from her having ground her teeth twenty or thirty years ago" – she knows that this grinding had a painful effect upon the family, and a formative effect on her own fiction. Obviously drawing from her mother's life in several books, she has commented: "I think she finds it terribly hard to read my books because there's so much that she recognizes and yet it's all slightly twisted. It must be very hard for her to know what I meant and what I didn't mean – difficult for anyone."[10]

In spite of the difficulties of their relationship, Margaret was, she believes, her mother's "favorite child" who profited from her mother's high expectation of her, and they continued to see each other frequently until Mrs Drabble's death in 1984. Because of her mother's example, though, Margaret was left with the impression throughout her adolescence that "adult life seemed to be incredibly depressing," and throughout her life she has looked for "mother figures" and established "imitative relationships"[11] with other women – the first model for which was her relationship with her older sister Antonia Susan, whom she used to "tag around after" when they were children. This sister is A. S. Byatt, the noted novelist and critic, and for a time senior lecturer in English and American literature at University College, London.

Margaret is the second child in a family of four children which includes a younger sister Helen, an art historian, and a much younger brother who is a barrister. She points out that her family was of the same size and constitution as the Brontë

21

family and that, like the Brontës, they were all commonly interested in writing, and in their childhood composed stories together.[12] This shared, childhood, Brontëan, imaginary world is recreated in A. S. Byatt's novel *The Game* (1967), a book about two sisters, Cassandra and Julia Corbett. And among the most interesting kinds of relationship in both sisters' works are those between two women – sisters, cousins, friends – relationships which grow in part out of the real relationship of these literary sisters. Likewise, then, Margaret's younger-sister perspective pervades her fiction from her first novel, *A Summer Bird-Cage* (1963), in which Sarah Bennett "liberates" herself from the domination her elder, Louise, holds over her, through Drabble's repeated portrayals of women who look to another for a model of how to live. Jane Gray in *The Waterfall* (1969), for example, says her cousin Lucy "was my sister, my fate, my example: her effect on me was incalculable." Not only does she model her life on her cousin's, she has an affair with her husband. A. S. Byatt writes much more explicitly about the potent rivalry implicit in such sisterly bonds and about the difficulties of maintaining a separate self in a shared, merged experience. The bond in *The Game* is such that the elder sister, Cassandra, commits suicide over her novelist sister's expropriation of herself and her world. To call these sisterly relationships potent, then, is no over-statement.

Both sisters take pains to point out that the characters in their fictions are often based on quite different women and not their sisters at all (Margaret, for example, claims that one model is a friend with whom she has had a "passionately complex" relationship, "much more satisfying"[13] than the one with her sister). Yet the sibling pattern of relating, set in childhood, is, I would argue, very important. Both Margaret and Antonia are exceedingly reluctant to talk about their relationship, being deferential and cautious with one another, annoyed that they are so often linked, anxious not to interfere with one another's work and privacy. More than many writers Margaret Drabble is particularly sensitive to the way that fiction can impinge upon the privacy of others:

I think that it is a terribly difficult area, and obviously there are many good things that one would like to deal with but for various reasons one never could. I find that there are things that are too close, or that are too painful, or that are too personal, or that would be treachery to another person, and you can't use them, however good they are.[14]

It is an issue she writes about in one of her novels, *The Millstone* (1965), and which Byatt portrays vividly in *The Game*. Readers too must respect the guarded privacy of the Drabble sisters, yet their works imply a great deal about female bonding in life and in literature, and about how female identity and creativity are complicated and enriched by a sisterly "other."

Their lives and careers have been strikingly parallel. Both went to The Mount school and then to Newnham College, Cambridge, on scholarships. Both were brilliant graduates in English literature. Both got married, had children, divorced and eventually remarried. Both became novelists, critics, essayists, lecturers, social commentators. They have written at times on similar topics, such as Byatt's *Wordsworth and Coleridge in Their Time* (1973) and Drabble's *Wordsworth* (1969), and their works – both fictional and non-fictional – can be read sometimes as implicit commentaries on one another. The controlled intellectuality informing all of Byatt's work contrasts sharply with Drabble's informality. While having much in common, the Drabble sisters are different in temperament and deliberately went separate ways. At Cambridge Margaret was active in drama and moved in somewhat different circles then and later from those of her more academic sister, who after Cambridge went to Bryn Mawr in the United States "because of needing space to be myself. . . . It is . . . hard to have shared memories with another writer. So much of art is a transmutation of memory, and this needs to be private not communal, or it is in danger of being destroyed."[15] While Byatt returned to Oxford for postgraduate research on allegory in Renaissance literature, Drabble deliberately veered away from an academic career. She got married right after university in June 1960 to Clive Swift, a Cambridge graduate in English, who became a leading actor.

The couple spent their first year of marriage in Stratford-on-Avon as members of the Royal Shakespeare Company. When pregnant with her first child, however, Drabble gave up her acting career and found writing more compatible with her role as young wife and mother. The couple had three children before they separated in 1972 and divorced in 1975. Margaret Drabble has for years lived with her children in a comfortable house in Hampstead. While she has been known to make skeptical comments about marriage ("I don't know why one gets married"[16]), she has always been very positive about motherhood: "I see motherhood in such positive terms that I feel almost embarrassed to state it. I think it's the greatest joy in the world. But it is also a very personal thing. I just happen to like it."[17] "I certainly feel the mother–child relationship is a great salvation and is an image of unselfish love, which is very hard to get in an adult relationship, I think, if not impossible."[18] "Having children gives you an access to an enormous common store of otherness about other people. This is how I learned that other people really existed."[19] She claims that a positive model for mothering was Mrs Swift, her mother-in-law, who created a demonstrably loving family home which contrasted so strikingly with her own inhibited one.[20] Drabble's credible portrayals of the mother–child bond have earned her the title, not always flatteringly meant, "novelist of maternity," and have drawn female readers empathetically to her work. Furthermore, subjects related to child-rearing have been topics of some of her feature articles and occasional writing. She has felt compelled to protect her children from fictional invasions of privacy, saying she can use them only as "decor." Her most recent novel, *The Middle Ground* (1980), however, is dedicated to her daughter, "my darling Becky," from whom she claims to have taken "quite a lot of copy": "It's about being a mother to teenage children and knowing that the children are going to be gone any minute now. And you've done all the things in your life you meant to do – what next?"[21]

What came next for Margaret Drabble was her marriage, in September 1982, to the distinguished biographer and man of letters, Michael Holroyd. Although she is very modest about her allegedly "non-scholar" status, she is a distinguished woman of letters in her own right, making this a literary marriage of note. One wonders if both her marriage and her mammoth recent project, the re-editing of the *Oxford Companion to English Literature*, will have the effect of increasing the "literariness" of her own creative work, which has until now been characterized by such a fertile tension between the traditional and the modern, the literary and the experiential.

*

In fact, one of the striking things about recent British fiction in general has been its willingness to summon up the past tradition of the British novel as a sufficient and usable past, capable of being questioningly adapted to late twentieth-century circumstances. Margaret Drabble was explicit early in her career about her identification with the great nineteenth-century English tradition, and showed herself disdainful of the more ambiguous modes of modernism and postwar experimentalism: "I'd rather be at the end of a dying tradition which I admire than at the beginning of a tradition which I deplore," she told a BBC interviewer in 1967. Like quite a number of British writers, she came under the influence of F. R. Leavis, who taught her at Cambridge in the 1950s, and was inculcated with the centrality of his "Great Tradition" of the novel: "I admire Leavis enormously. I'm sure he's right about the people whom he admires, and the Great Tradition is what I believe in as a novelist. I mean, his preoccupations are my preoccupations." His preoccupations were with the novel as a social and moral form, generating a tradition of human responsibility; and she shares his belief that the novel is "the one bright book of life," that fiction at its best is distinguished by

25

what Leavis called "a vital capacity for experience, a kind of reverent openness before life, and a marked moral intensity."

What Drabble found harder to accept, especially as a fledgling writer, were the uncompromising aesthetic standards that Leavis advanced, and his dismissal of the contemporary scene as an insufficient source for serious fiction: "It was so destructive: the standards were so high. . . . So I think he has affected me deeply, and it was just good luck that he didn't stop me completely."[22] This crisis is very recognizable among younger British writers, for whom Leavis in the 1950s was a powerful influence; and so is the doubt she has expressed about some of Leavis's specific selection of great writers. She has questioned his emphasis on Jane Austen, whose "social snobbery" is to her coercive, and Henry James, whose emphasis on rarified consciousness she finds restrictive. Her own sense of the tradition has undoubtedly been a good deal more capacious: "The writers I admire are people who strive to retain their links with the community and not indulge their own consciousness to such a degree that they become rarified."[23] One judicious addition she, like John Wain, has made to the Great Tradition is Arnold Bennett, whom Leavis found "beneath contempt." On this Drabble comments: "if people like that are beneath contempt, why should one ever dare to begin?"[24]

Bennett's attraction for Drabble is not just for critical reasons; she suspects, she admits in her biography of him (p. 24), that he is a distant relative. But it is above all because "he has a great respect for ordinary life and ordinary people. . . . And because of this grounding in knowledge of ordinary people, which Virginia Woolf, for example, did not have, Arnold Bennett tells you things that Virginia Woolf simply didn't know." She shares his respect for the "ordinary." Her documentation of manners and morals, texture and detail, contains a recognition, drawn from the line of the British novel, that within the world of the ordinary are fundamental social and historical processes the novelist must grasp, and what she most admires in writers as different as Bennett and Words-worth is their "transfiguration of the everyday . . . this quality of writing about an everyday incident making it profoundly emblematic,"[25] a quality her own work possesses. Like Bennett, she attends to material spaces – the houses which are as much a part of her characters as their bodies,[26] the landscapes and cityscapes indissolubly grafted onto their beings. Valuing the social breath of Bennett's works, she finds that Virginia Woolf's circumscribed fictional space leaves out a great deal of the world and human experience.

In all this, she is explicitly siding with Bennett in the great division of materialist realism and modernism that was explored by Virginia Woolf in her famous essay "Mr Bennett and Mrs Brown" (1924). This was part of the temper of her generation; like a good number of other British novelists since the 1950s, she has reacted against the class-bound literary and social milieu of prewar Bloomsbury and broken sharply away in many respects from modernist forebears: James, Joyce, Dorothy Richardson, as well as Woolf. One way of seeing the novel, and very familiar in Britain in the 1950s and 1960s, was to view it as poised between the two poles of realism and formalism – allegiance on one hand to referential social and historical expressiveness, on the other to formal and symbolic force. Drabble joined those who emphasized the first and helped re-direct fiction toward social and moral realism. She agrees with Iris Murdoch who argues in "Against Dryness" (*Encounter*, 1961) that the novelist's aim should not be to produce a dry crystalline work but rather to engage with "the real impenetrable human person. That this person is substantial, impenetrable, indefinable, and valuable is after all the fundamental tenet of Liberalism." Drabble, if with a rather different result, also values that liberal humanist tradition, which has been a matter for much speculation in postwar British fiction. For her, like Murdoch, the artist, rather than choosing romantic isolation or aestheticism, must deal in "degrees of freedom" and engage with the reality of character and the substantive nature of the world; Drabble's work is hence deeply rooted in the line of British socio-moral fiction. Perhaps it is most fundamentally about playing one's proper part in the human community:

> We are not free from our past, we are never free of the claims of others, and we ought not wish to be (Existential thought, and emphasis on the *acte gratuite*, has always seemed to me a very inadequate way of looking at life). We are all part of a long inheritance, a human community in which we must play our proper part.[27]

Indeed, a distinctive note of accommodation, self-sacrifice, and recognition of limitations and obligations – irritating to some readers – characterizes her moral stance. It is not incidental that houses and landscapes do play such an important role in her fiction: the search for one's place – a suitable moral and human habitation – is the compelling genesis of her art, and in this she is linked to the temperate romanticism of Wordsworth, Austen, Arnold and George Eliot rather than to the romantic extremism of Blake, Byron or the Brontës, or the aesthetic and social isolation of the modernists – or indeed the totalitarian and dehumanizing spirit of some of the post-modernists. A writer Drabble particularly resembles in her yoking of Victorian values and modern sensibility is E. M. Forster. She, like Forster, grapples with how to live a life of integrated humanism in the face of the growing complexities and dehumanization of modern existence. Her work, like his, is concerned with "connecting" the personal and the social, the classes that make up a society, the land and human habitation. Like Forster, she shows a capacity for passionate romanticism balanced with, and finally outweighed by, common sense. Like him, she yearns for greater connectedness: momentary visions of seeing life steadily and seeing it whole are for both writers consolations for human fragility and incompleteness.

The contemporary novelists Drabble most frequently mentions as those she feels affinities to are Angus Wilson, Doris Lessing, and the Americans Saul Bellow and Mary McCarthy –

novelists who, like herself, are not for the most part considered experimental or post-modernist. These novelists have in fact sometimes been viewed as reactionary, or at least out of step with the experimental developments of the modern novel. Along with other contemporaries, they appear to some observers to be clinging to a view of human nature and causality which depends on a social order and an epistemology no longer tenable. Bernard Bergonzi in the *Situation of the Novel* (1979), for example, argues that the English novel is "no longer novel" – has lost its stylistic dynamism, settled for a realistic sameness, a reaching back to older models which are inappropriate to the times. Yet, as Malcolm Bradbury has convincingly argued in a number of essays, English novelists have not been immune to "the waves of fictional revisionism" going on elsewhere, and "the attempt to mediate between the traditional realism and humanism of the nineteenth-century novel and the epistemological problems of fiction in our time [has] been of considerable importance in English fiction, and has given it something of a distinctive character."[28] In short, there is in contemporary British fiction an eclectic resynthesis, a revived and not entirely simplistic liberalism and realism; it is part of its force, its liveliness and its sense of crisis. Margaret Drabble shares with a number of her contemporaries this mediating position between the traditional and the modern, the Great Tradition and other traditions, the literary and the real.

A moral and aesthetic dependence on literary forebears – an anxiety of influence – is viewed with unease by some commentators, however, including Drabble's sister, A. S. Byatt: "Respect for the tradition of the realistic novel is apparently a very rooted fact . . . and many novelists now seem to feel that they exist in some uneasy relation to the afterlife of these texts." Emphasizing the "symbiotic relationship" between old realism and new experiment, she is concerned with the "ambiguous power and restrictiveness of the tradition."[29] Likewise some critics of Margaret Drabble have been dissatisfied with this "literariness" as it manifests itself as a pattern of allusion and guidance in the writing of her novels. Elizabeth Fox-Genovese, for example, isolates a "dualism at the heart of Drabble's work," a discernible split, a tension between "female self-consciousness" and "artistic self-consciousness." Her novels have a "superficially casual, conversational tone" in which is embedded "a tremendous overlay of highly crafted imagery . . . a linguistic texture, a network of signs that adds a neomannerist illusion of depth to the otherwise willfully innocent and everyday prose style." Fox-Genovese claims: "it is hard to avoid the suspicion that she is speaking in two languages at once – that of a female being on the one hand, that of double-first Cambridge essays on the other." I agree that Drabble's novels are considerably more crafted than their surface lucidity might at first suggest. While Fox-Genovese criticizes her for being "culturally aware to the point of trendiness" and calls her skillful metaphors and allusions a "literary veneer,"[30] I believe that Drabble's metaphorical, allusive language – her "artistic self-consciousness" – contributes considerable subtlety and depth to her work.

Her fiction is located within, enriched by and played off against the literary language, traditions and characters she knows so well. "Naturally," says Drabble, "what I've read is as much a part of what I think as the people that I meet and the problems that I encounter. . . . So I don't see it as decorating one's books with literature. I think that literature is a part of life."[31] *The Waterfall* (1969), for example, rewrites women's stories, lives, and fantasies: the fiction is drawn against a culturally shared tradition of "womenslore." Jane Gray, conscious of the literary and historical doubles who precede her – Maggie Tulliver, Jane Eyre, Charlotte Brontë, Jane Austen, Lady Jane Grey, and the tragic heroines of the sentimental novel, to name only some – tries to live and write her version of the perennial Sleeping Beauty love story. Furthermore, this literary reality may have a potency that mere factual reality cannot duplicate: "Which was Charlotte Brontë's man, the one she created and wept for and longed for, or the poor curate that had her and killed her, her sexual measure, her sexual match?" (*W*, p. 89). For Margaret Drabble, too, both the literature she

30

reads and the literature she writes are very potent engagements with the real.

While her work draws strength from literary contexts, it is also grounded in real experience, particularly women's experience; and it is here that feminist perspectives — but not modernist ones — are most evident. She has commented on how profoundly she was affected by reading Simone de Beauvoir's *The Second Sex* while she was at Cambridge: "This seemed to me to be wonderful material and so important to me as a person. It was material that nobody had used and I could use and nobody had ever used as far as I could see as I would use it."[32] In drawing inspiration and example from writers such as Simone de Beauvoir, the early Doris Lessing and Mary McCarthy, rather than Virginia Woolf and Dorothy Richardson, Drabble breaks here too from the modernist tradition which would make of both novelistic and psychic female space a deathly safe "inner" place. As Elaine Showalter has astutely commented:

> In her fiction but supremely in *A Room of One's Own*, Woolf is the architect of female space, a space that is both sanctuary and prison. Through their windows, her women observe a more violent masculine world in which their own anger, rebellion, and sexuality can be articulated at a safe remove. . . . "The woman writer is urged to be as 'Woolfian' as possible," according to Joyce Carol Oates — that is, to be subjective, and yet to transcend her femaleness, to write exquisitely about inner space and leave the messy brawling novels to men. . . . In one sense Woolf's female aesthetic is an extension of her view of women's social role: receptivity to the point of self-destruction, creative synthesis to the point of exhaustion and sterility. . . . Refined of its essences, abstracted from its physicality and denied any action, Woolf's vision of womanhood is as deadly as it is disembodied. The ultimate room of one's own is the grave.[33]

Drabble's early novels, in fact, can be read as penetrating exposures of the sanctuary and the prison of such prototypically female spaces, as well as struggles toward her own right to larger fictional space.

Locked inside their heads, her early characters are narcissistically preoccupied with their appearance, with the bodies which they use as deceptively misleading façades and barriers against intrusion. Their houses are usually extensions of themselves and protective retreats from external realities. These first-person narrators are for the most part intelligent, educated, and naturally fluent in the discourses of literature, psychology, and contemporary culture. Yet their explanations of themselves are fragmentary and sometimes clearly inadequate. Their verbalizations are often classic defenses against unpleasant self-revelation. The resulting tension between surface and meaning gives to Drabble's novels an unresolved, exploratory quality that draws readers into conjecture and speculation about the unarticulated, the unexamined, the unexplained. Drabble's fiction at its best is a virtual "double-voiced discourse"[34] exemplifying the tension experienced by many contemporary women who are struggling to define themselves within a patriarchal frame of reference. The strength of these characterizations stems from her own unresolved questioning and her experiences of living in what she has termed the "unchartered world" of modern female identity:

> We do not want to resemble the women of the past, but where is our future? This is precisely the question that many novels written by women are trying to answer: some in comic terms, some in tragic, some in speculative. We live in an unchartered world, as far as manners and morals are concerned, we are having to make up our morality as we go. Our subject matter is enormous, there are whole new patterns to create.[35]

Although feminists like Ellen Cronan Rose would like her to write "an unequivocally feminist blueprint,"[36] Drabble does not in her life or in her fiction advocate a feminist overthrow of the patriarchal order. Rather, she is a good-humored realist, who mediates between "male" and "female" social, cultural, and literary heritages, producing a resonant fiction which is prototypically of her time, her place, *and* her gender.

Recently Drabble has written poignantly of the forgotten tradition of minor women writers she unearthed while working on her new edition of the *Oxford Companion to English Literature*.[37] Furthermore, she has said of her belated discovery of Virginia Woolf that she feels as if she had been influenced by Woolf, even though she hadn't actually read her.[38] After reading *A Room of One's Own*, for example, she said, "I felt so in sympathy with everything she said about the tradition of women's writing and where it is going. And I know that's what I'm part of."[39] Not only has Drabble now written perceptively on Woolf's work, but her latest novel, *The Middle Ground* (1980), is both parody of and tribute to Woolf and the female experience and traditions that link them.

Discussing with David Leon Higdon the usual 10- to 12-month time frame in her novels, Drabble notes both that this is also about the time it takes for her to write a book (and to produce a child – and her first three books were written while she was expecting her three children) and that "the idea of plotting a novel which is going to take me five years is impossible, because I would have changed very much in five years and my world would have changed and would have lost everything." Because she does not stay in the same spot, her fiction is constantly nourished by her own personal development. As a result, Drabble perhaps more than any other contemporary British woman novelist has the opportunity to produce a distinctly female work which surpasses gender limitations. She has said many times how much she admires and strives to emulate George Eliot: for her range of subject matter, her social consciousness, her breadth. She mentions *Middlemarch* as a likely model for her next book, particularly its use of the omniscient narrator and the interconnected articulation of society – a kind of novel Drabble has approached in her more recent fiction.

These broader, omnisciently narrated books of her later

period – *The Realms of Gold, The Ice Age, The Middle Ground* – continue to be, in many ways, double-voiced, mediating, equivocal. Even when Drabble seems to be adopting traditional novelistic conventions, she is, in fact, adapting them, for she cannot reproduce the old sureties which often lay behind narrative conventions in the hands of eighteenth- and nineteenth-century writers – and she knows it. She uses them with playful and ironic detachment. As Angus Wilson has perceptively said, "She presses against the outer edges of the realistic mode with such respectful serious teasing . . . that the simple or the hasty or the prejudiced . . . see only her competence, sincerity, and readability, and give only ordinary consideration to what we mistakenly class as ordinary work."[40]

The playfully omniscient and obtrusive narrative voice of her later fiction calls attention to itself and has, in fact, provoked adverse critical commentary. Morton P. Levitt, for example, claims: "Her words speak of a worldview that is surely appropriate to a post-Modernist writer; the points of view of her novels are deliberately and grossly pre-Modernist. Her sense of irony is at no time directed at this paradoxical split . . . she wills to out-Trollope Trollope. . . . This is Trollope revisited, to be sure, but, in the context of a new time for which his vision and narrative technique are woefully unsuited, it is also Trollope demeaned."[41] I think that she does direct irony against this "split" between form and content. Such coy and playful remarks as "Invent a more suitable ending if you can," such admissions as "Omniscience has its limits" must certainly be viewed as ironic. While seemingly invited into a familiar rapport, readers must remain cautious. Drabble skillfully interjects modernist uncertainties into the convention of authorial omniscience.

Margaret Drabble is not at all immune to the way that structuralist and post-structuralist ways of perceiving are altering basic presuppositions about language, about the way we construct our world, about the individual and society. Her fiction, like that of her contemporaries, records unease and disorientation. In her more recent fiction she portrays the individual's struggle for self-creation and self-definition within culturally shared fantasies, ideologies, definitions, and values. The individual may be, as Anthony Keating in *The Ice Age* (1977) suspects, no more than a "weed upon the tide of history," doomed to enact a drama which differs only in particulars from other members of his or her class and generation. Similarly, *The Middle Ground* equivocates between personal and national "midlife transition." Drabble's most recent work shows the gradual erosion of the class system, of the provincial insularity of the English, of the distinctions between high and low culture, and the gradual dominance of the trends, fads, and common experiences of mass urban culture. Similarly, it depicts a weakening of traditional norms in manners and morals: liberal humanism is replaced by communal and personal uncertainty and disorientation. Failing to order experience into clear patterns of meaning, both the characters and the author face "shapeless diversity." If there is a sense of fatigue with the mere repeating of predictable and depleted material, with conventions no longer vital, it may be a reflection on the lack of dynamism in British life and culture itself, as Britain adjusts to its lessened role in world politics and culture, and to economic instability. This, at least, is what she implies in *The Ice Age*. She expresses there a vague belief – or perhaps hope – that "Britain will recover" and its writers be revitalized as they respond, after crossing the disorientating "middle ground," to the next phase of personal and communal development.

There is a deeply personal, honest, and exploratory quality about Margaret Drabble's work. She confronts the unknown and acknowledges her limitations – too readily, according to some readers. If at times it seems that she, like her characters, resorts to "muddling through" a fog of uncertainty and mystery, it is because she genuinely values the distinctly British traits of cheerful endurance and accommodation, but also because she is groping her way toward "truth." In so doing, she is, along with some of her contemporaries – John Fowles, Angus Wilson, Iris Murdoch, Doris Lessing, Anthony Burgess,

Muriel Spark, and others – also perceptibly changing and challenging the conventions and the epistemological assumptions of traditional realistic fiction, perhaps in spite of herself. I do not believe Margaret Drabble self-consciously sets out to be "double-voiced," equivocal or ambiguous. Rather, she "aims to be lucid": "I *hate* books which are deliberately confusing."[42] While seeking a moral and humanistic center and voice, her fiction necessarily reflects the contemporary world in its complexities and uncertainties. Her strength as a writer lies in the way she is attuned to her time, her place and herself even while she looks back to the past and the literary tradition for connections and guidance. Her intensified concern with social determinism and historical change has in some ways made her more of a realist, in other ways less of one. Like many serious novelists writing in Britain today, she displays in her work the problems of interpreting an estranging, contemporary society no longer easily domesticated by the novelist. Her very willingness to change as a novelist goes along with her sense of the novel as an open form, not a structure of certainty, a form capable of irresolution, of inconclusiveness, of a "feminine ending." Indeed, her openness to contingency, I believe, is very much related to her conscious working through the role of a serious contemporary woman writer who finds "There are whole new patterns to create." Margaret Drabble's career is a study of her progressive discovery of the possibilities of both the female voice and of the novel form itself. This book will chart the changing scope of her fiction from the early first-person narratives to the larger, ambitious novels of her "middle-ground."

2

BIRD-CAGES

It is not surprising that Margaret Drabble's early novels – focused as they were on the first-person narrations of sympathetic but self-engrossed female protagonists facing the crises and conflicts of modern domestic life – quickly earned her the ambiguous and sometimes troubling reputation of being a "women's novelist." The phrase easily takes on condescending overtones, and was associated with descriptions of her as "the novelist of maternity," whose work was devoted to "coping with frigidity and nappies." It was no great step from this to viewing her as a "middle-brow writer," whose books could be compared with "women's magazines such as *Nova* or the upgraded afternoon television soap operas."[43] The view of her as a novelist whose exploration of the daily lives of middle-class women is inherently trivial and disconnected from larger social and political matters has persisted, despite all evidence to the contrary. She herself has offered the most pointed refutation of this kind of disdain, which has come from both male and female critics:

> There is no point in sneering at women writers for writing of problems of sexual behaviour, of maternity, or gynaecology – those who feel the need to do it are actively engaged in creating a new pattern, a new blueprint. This area of personal relationships verges constantly on the political: it is not a narrow backwater of introversion, it is the main current

which is changing the daily quality of our lives. The truest advantage of being a woman writer now is that never before, perhaps, have women had so much to say, and so great a hope of speaking to some effect.[44]

For all the flippancy and humor with which her characters present themselves and for all the trivialities of their lives and concerns, beneath this surface Drabble is examining with subtlety and moral acuity the very tissue and structure of women's lives. She is not a simple perpetuator of "bourgeois feminism," popular culture, middle-class values, or indeed, simple views. From her first novel, *A Summer Bird-Cage* (1963), depicting Sarah Bennett's indecisiveness about how to shape her life given the bird-cage of female identity she sees played out in the lives of women around her, to her latest novel, *The Middle Ground* (1980), portraying Kate Armstrong's paralyzing mid-life crisis in which no satisfactory pattern of how to live emerges, Drabble has been exposing the social-political-spiritual paucity of traditional avenues of middle-class female self-fulfillment.

Part of the problem of reading Drabble's early novels is that they are a good deal more dense and more subtle than at first they appear. The surface lucidity of her early novels and the seeming candor of her first-person narrators have misled some readers into assuming that little critical distance separates the author and her narratives; the problem is an old one, common to first-person novels since *Moll Flanders*. So articulate and direct, so seemingly honest and confessional, the narrators invite readers into a familiar rapport, seduce them into thinking that they are thin personas of the author herself. Yet both individually and collectively these women must also, I believe, invite the readers' suspicions. With no simple separation of the author from the narrator, locating the "implied author" through the veils of the narrators' sometimes candid, sometimes smoothly defensive rhetoric is always problematical. This uncertainty, which draws readers into creative interaction with the text and subverts attempts to arrive at definitive assessments of the characters, gives Margaret Drabble's work its hidden complexity, distinguishing it from the popular women's fiction it deceptively resembles. From her comparatively slight first novel, *A Summer Bird-Cage*, Drabble's first-person characterizations grow in depth and subtlety, reaching their culmination in the portrait of Jane Gray in her most technically experimental narrative, *The Waterfall* (1969). While each of these narrators lives in a solipsistic world and uses her body as a decorative front and self-protective retreat from external realities, *The Waterfall* also records Jane Gray's very equivocal breaking out of the constricting bird-cage of female identity. It seems appropriate that this comes at a time when Drabble's novels are widening in theme, and moving away from the first to the third person. In fact before *The Waterfall* Drabble wrote her first third-person novel, *Jerusalem the Golden* (1967). But in this chapter I have chosen to group Drabble's first-person novels of the 1960s together, in order to get a clear view of her increasingly more sophisticated use of this narrative perspective.

*

In her first novel, *A Summer Bird-Cage* (1963), Drabble lays down the kind of style and situation that will characterize a number of her early novels. Sarah Bennett is a candid, breezy, confessional, humorous first person narrator who initially draws readers into a rapport, lulls them into intimacy, until the anomalies and omissions in her explanations effect some critical distance. Like Emma Evans, Rosamund Stacey, and Jane Gray to follow, Sarah is a young woman blessed with intelligence, good looks, articulateness, and humor, whose sense of expectation, aspiration, and promise is coupled with a disturbing lassitude, an inability to know what to do as a female person. Evidently inspired, like several of her books, by Simone de Beauvoir's *The Second Sex*, and taking its title from John Webster,[45] the novel is an exploration of the bird-cage of female identity played out for circumspect Sarah in the lives of the "over-educated" women "lacking a sense of vocation" who surround her.

Having recently come down from Oxford with a distinguished record, a First, Sarah thinks about the "classlessness and social dislocation that girls of my age and lack of commitments feel. I sat silent, amazed by the recognition of how much I missed community, and how deeply I felt my social loneliness. I had no colleagues, no neighbours, no family" (*SBC*, p. 96). Unable to commit herself to marriage or career, or even to envisage a future, she takes a filing job with the BBC and shares a flat with a college friend, Gill, who is separated from her husband. This temporary encampment and "the temporary pointlessness of our lives" provoke Sarah's comment: "Girls shouldn't share flats, but who else can they share them with?" (p. 99). Sarah is, at times, depressed over the shapelessness of women's lives, their vulnerability:

> I looked horrifyingly pregnable, somehow, at that moment: I looked at myself in fascination, thinking how unfair it was, to be born with so little defence, like a soft snail without a shell. Men are all right, they are defined and enclosed, but we in order to live must be open and raw to all comers. What happens otherwise is worse than what happens normally, the embroidery and the children and the sagging mind. I felt doomed to defeat. I felt all women were doomed. (pp. 28–9)

Other women are models or rivals to be emulated or overcome.

Sarah is obsessed with her older sister Louise, to whom she is bound in a competitive, uncommunicative, yet symbiotic relationship. Repulsed by Louise's coveting of material possessions and social smartness, Sarah, however, understands neither Louise nor the part of herself which is like her sister. The novel turns on Sarah's liberation from the domination that Louise has held over her. As a young child Sarah would hang around Louise, only to be shunned. At Oxford she learns with the help of a friend that Louise "forced me into grudgingness," into defensiveness, into an "almost whining position" (p. 20). Now, with a certain amount of hard-won independence, she balks at lowering her defenses: "I didn't want to talk female intimacies. Not with her" (p. 28). Gradually, however, as Louise becomes humanized in Sarah's eyes, Sarah frees herself from her younger-sister intimidation by Louise's older-sister imperiousness. At the end of the book, Sarah can finally, tentatively, cast Louise into the role of friend and confidante, rather than symbiotic and resented older sibling. This more adult perspective on her sister may in turn clarify some of the perplexities of middle-class womanhood with which she is struggling.

Other models include Gill, Sarah's room-mate, whose early marriage to Tony has already disintegrated, illustrating for Sarah the folly of blindly leaping into a marriage of love. The opposite, a life of domestic order and harmony, is portrayed in the marriage of Stephanie and Michael, for which Sarah has both envy and contempt – for she feels that such a harmonious set-up will not be her lot, and that, in fact, she wants more than such middle-class coziness. Simone, who manages a life of elegant and refined singleness, is a solitary feminist existentialist;[46] she "moves through a strange impermanent world . . . totally divorced from the world of sensations and rhythms" in which Sarah lives: "With her I sensed a wholly willed, a wholly undetermined life" (pp. 70–1). Extravagantly admiring Simone and thinking of her as an idealized older sister, Sarah is, in fact, much closer to her real sister Louise in strengths and limitations, outlook and prospects, than to Simone or anyone else.

One must note both the extraordinary potential and the limited aspiration of these Bennett sisters, who recall and vividly contrast with Jane Austen's Bennet sisters in *Pride and Prejudice*. The options for these modern Bennetts are so much more extensive: it is not merely a matter of marrying well, but of charting one's own identity in a changing social world, though with this new freedom comes a moral ambiguity and gender uncertainty quite unknown to Austen's sisters. Keenly interested in literature and writing, Sarah occupies herself with a dead-end job and preoccupies herself with parties, looking

41

only to be amused and not seriously engaged in dialogue with others. She wryly comments that perhaps the only accomplishment her education has bestowed on her is the ability to think in quotations. She rejects a university career because: "You can't be a sexy don. It's all right for men, being learned and attractive, but for a woman it's a mistake. It detracts from the essential seriousness of the business" (pp. 183–4). Like all of Drabble's women, she values inordinately her appearance and sexual attractiveness. The horror of horrors for both Sarah and Louise is their cousin Daphne, whose excessive plainness and dowdiness seems the worst fate that could ever befall a woman. Yet what do they do with their advantages? While Sarah claims to want "the whole world" (p. 70) and to be, like her sister, one of the "predatory" females who lives in the reflection of the lesser "herbivores" (pp. 164–5) such as Daphne, she is strangely limited in what she envisages as the world, and so is her sister.

Louise had tried to "force marriage into a new mould" by marrying money and choosing adultery, thereby reversing a previously male "tradition" of such extramarital arrangements. After Stephen catches Louise with her lover in the bathtub and throws her out of the house, Louise confesses to Sarah that she has had enough of her marriage to Stephen Halifax, thoroughly sick is she of "what a morass of duplicity that man is. . . . God, what a fool I was, what fools women are, what fools middle-class girls are to expect other people to respect the same gods as themselves and E. M. Forster" (p. 201). But this high-minded rhetoric comes strangely out of the mouth of Louise, who herself cynically and coldly exploits her marital relationship. Casting Stephen as the stagey and unredeemed villain too easily both diminishes Louise's moral culpability and simplifies the complex gender-related issues involved in her marital "bargain." Moreover, Louise's lover John, literally waiting in the wings, is too conveniently able to supply love, money, and Oxford-trained moral niceties. Louise is not made to face the limitations of her self-centered middle-class aspirations.

What saves the novel is the honesty and acuity with which Sarah comments on the texture of her life. More ambitious than Louise, more thoughtful about the alternatives of female identity, she is none the less curiously flattered when perceived by a casual male acquaintance as belonging to a class of "high-powered women." "High powered" is what she aspires to be, without really knowing what that means. Both sisters perceive themselves as being "serious" and "moral" without much justification. Sarah disdains the political activism of Stephanie and Michael, for example, claiming to believe in the possibility of personal rather than political change, and neither sister gives much thought to social and metaphysical questions of any sort, beyond Sarah's egotistical gratitude for being unfairly blessed: "I do feel perpetually the double-edged guilt and glory of having so much, so much abundance" (p. 167). Sarah thinks that perhaps "greater gifts" carry a "greater duty to society," yet she gives little thought to that duty.

Her lovely female body is also an isolated space, nourished by only fleeting intimacies, until she belatedly interjects her fiancé into the novel:

I now find myself compelled to relate a piece of information which I decided to withhold, on the grounds that it was irrelevant, but I realize increasingly that nothing is irrelevant. I meant to keep myself out of this story, which is a laugh, really, I agree: I see however that in failing to disclose certain facts I made myself out to be some sort of *voyeuse*, and I am too vain to leave anyone with the impression that the lives of others interest me more than my own. So I hasten, belatedly, to say that all this time I have been writing about I was in love with somebody quite outside this story, so far outside it that thousands of miles separate him and it. His name is Francis. We were in love for our last year at Oxford, most inseparably in love. I felt as though he carried me around in his pocket. At the end of the year, our final year, he, being a great scholar, was awarded a Commonwealth scholarship to go and study political theory at Harvard.

He said he wouldn't go. I said he should. I suppose we quarrelled. (p. 73)

Interrupting the narrative for such admissions is a technique Drabble will later refine and use with technical skill in *The Waterfall*, but its artistic function here is less controlled and certain. While one can take what Sarah says at face value, seeing this revelation as part of the personal, confessional style of the narrative,[47] we may be suspicious of Sarah's explanation – especially in the light of *The Garrick Year*, *The Millstone*, and *The Waterfall*, where other first-person narrators deal out various sophistic explanations and rationalizations for their sexual and marital abstinence and inhibition.

This ideal absent lover conveniently prevents Sarah both from having to deal with sexuality in her narrative and from having definitely to place herself within or without the birdcage of marriage. Their relationship has been tested only in the self-enclosed world of Oxford, authenticated only through hazily sentimental terms in the novel. Furthermore, Sarah's comments on their relationship at the end of the novel are highly ambiguous. On the one hand, she implies that her life has been in a limbo-like state during Francis's absence and that she will resume it when he returns, seeming to support "those stupid home truths about a woman being nothing without a man" (p. 187); this is a recapitulation to the traditional role, even though she earlier more confidently asserted that "the days are over, thank God, when a woman justifies her existence by marrying" (p. 74). On the other hand, she also implies that she has changed, and that this change may have altered her relationship with Francis. The nature of that change is uncertain to Sarah and to the reader. She may "marry a don," or may become a sexy don herself. She may not share Louise's limited sense of how to live as a woman, or still be locked in the same bird-cage of possibilities. This irresolution is very typically Drabblesque. Contrary to her characters' and her readers' "impulse to seize on one moment as the whole, one aspect as the total view, one attitude as a revelation" (p. 206), Drabble's novels – in spite of their surface lucidity – often maintain an unresolved tension between opposing views and possibilities.

While the focus of *A Summer Bird-Cage* is narrow, Drabble has in this novel captured the sense of drift and dislocation that women just leaving university often feel. While the events which preoccupy Sarah may seem trivial, the point is that so too typically are women's lives trivial and undefined at this stage. The inability to undertake significant action, or to connect with anything larger than the self, or to reach out of the confining space of one's own private consciousness is for Drabble's women increasingly a psychological and ultimately a moral problem.

*

Drabble's second novel, *The Garrick Year* (1964), is again narrow in scope: a retrospective look at a few months in the life of Emma Evans, a young wife and mother of two children who grudgingly spends a year with her actor-husband and a theatre group out of London. But its first-person characterization of Emma is complex, resonant and suggestive; what makes this book rich, like the others, is the way the narrator complicates and makes ambiguous the events and textures of her world. Like other Drabble heroines, Emma lives a solipsistic life behind her carefully cultivated social front, but with the reader she is disarmingly candid, even flippant, about her situation. At first she arouses our sympathy as a victim of male will, as she attempts to keep her composure to prevent her husband's verbal demands upsetting her nursing baby's oral ones, and as she gives up the chance of a career as a television newsreader in order to go with her husband to Hereford:

> I could hardly believe that marriage was going to deprive me of this too. It had already deprived me of so many things which I had childishly overvalued: my independence, my income, my twenty-two-inch waist, my sleep, most of my friends, who had deserted me on account of David's insults, a whole string of finite things, and many more indefinite attributes, like hope and expectation. (*GY*, p. 10)

But soon one sees that, as with Sarah, there are disturbing anomalies in Emma's view of herself, her attitude to conflicts, her sense of herself as a woman.

In common with the heroines in Drabble's other books, Emma has around her women who also play out a dialectic of female possibility that none the less offers no satisfactory pattern of self. Mary Scott, her school-friend, exemplifies the middle-class values in which Emma has been trained: quiet good taste, refinement, intelligence and respectability. Sophy Brent, an aspiring actress, is by contrast flashy, shallow, self-centered, vulgar, loose in morals and stupid. Yet Emma admits to preferring Sophy, and one part of her seeks out what she represents. She candidly tells the reader she has "aspirations towards gloss" (p. 11), that "my tastes are shallow, my life is shallow, and I like anonymity, change and fame" (p. 69). Yet Emma is too discerning not to see through gloss; in fact, she is bored and annoyed by Sophy and the theatrical set around her husband. Emma is often mistaken for an actress herself, though, and the theatrical implications of her behavior are many. She plays to an audience, watching their reactions from behind the distancing role she's adopted; the job of television newsreader attracts her because it would, she says, project her "face of quite startling and effective gravity" across the nation's screens, and indulge her "passion for facts and mild yearning for notoriety" (p. 10). She sees television's way of turning life into artifice, sanitizing it, holding it in false stasis, yet wants to be a "bland-faced" player in this make-believe (p. 12). The deceits of contemporary success, the ambiguities of performance, help generate the book's texture of moral anxiety and irony.

Emma adopts a pose strikingly eccentric, remotely alienating, as her male double Julian testifies: "Everyone's scared to death of you, Emma. Did you know that?" (p. 141). She recognizes the irony herself: only by establishing this "bleak distance" from others can she gain their respect and a place of distinction, for when she is seen in her traditional female role – being pregnant, or holding her infant son – she is ignored and underestimated: "I noticed that Sophy was not bothering to watch me. I knew why: it was because I had a baby on my knee. You underestimate me, my girl, I said to myself" (p. 36). Wanting Sophy's "respect and dislike" (p. 61) more than her affection, she can have them only by demonstrating she has aspirations beyond the traditional female roles. Her appearance is an "obstinate artifact of life" (p. 37); so too are the houses she carefully selects and imbues with her own deliberate unconventionality, using her domestic space to explore and explicate herself. She chooses the house in Hereford, for example, for its "dignity" and unconventionality rather than comfort and convenience, carefully covering its cheap and utilitarian furniture "with my carefully accumulated objects and scraps of tattered and embroidered cloth" (p. 43) – and so making her home, like her body, an eccentrically decorated exterior. Wyndham Farrah calls her "house proud," and she indeed prides herself on her efficiency and control within the household, seeing herself congenitally incapable of the lapse her husband and the hired help Pascal commit when they fail to notice the gas is on one evening. And, significantly, her household is threatened just at the point when her personal control is; the incident occurs when she is out with Wyndham Farrah.

Her affair with Farrah is a challenge to her domestic self – a courting of danger, as, she claims, her marriage first was, for marrying David "seemed to be the most frightful, unlikely thing I could possibly do. . . . I did not want an easy life, I wanted something precipitous" (p. 25). Yet Emma, both in her marriage and in her affair, actually prevents anything truly precipitous from happening. The marriage is characterized by her oppressive self-sacrificing domesticity and her compulsive orderliness, which she recognizes as defenses against the very chaos she claims to desire. Similarly she characterizes their infrequent sexual encounters as "legalized rape." She maintains such devastating self-control in her affair that it generates no passion in herself and little in Farrah, beyond the fascination of the difficult: "Trying to get a kiss out of you is like

47

trying to get blood out of a stone," he complains (p. 132), and ruefully remarks that she is a woman who in more ways than one likes *hors d'oeuvres* rather than the main course.[48]

Emma enjoys the tantalizing flirtation, the danger and the trappings, but rebuffs the more serious sexual overtones; she is more enchanted with the idea of "having an affair" than the affair she is having. She watches with some bemusement her own responses, an audience to her own play-acting: "When I reached my bedroom, I stared into the mirror of that hideous dressing-table at my own chilly face and said aloud 'Wyndham' to see what the word would sound like, let loose from the furtive hutch of my mind. It sounded bloody silly, and my face and lips intoning it looked ridiculous" (p. 110). Her rationality functions as a chill; she tries to be infatuated with her lover but remains detached and observing: "I hung on his every word and gesture: every compliment enchanted me, every glance unclothed me, and yet I could not deceive myself that it was him, himself, that I liked. For one thing, he was a frightful namedropper . . ." (p. 112).

Like many a nineteenth-century literary heroine, and many a twentieth-century romantic one, Emma's crisis of resolving reason and feeling is tested in her inability to respond to the natural, either inside or outside herself. We see this in the scene when she and Wyndham go to look at his aunt's house, and she is totally unnerved by the landscape, a reality outside the narrow human control within which she has tried to live. It is appropriate that the apple she stumbles on is rotten; temptation decays before she can bring herself to taste the forbidden fruit. Yet she craves the freedom from all control and limitation. Latent masochistic and self-destructive wishes, coupled neurotically with their reverse, have characterized the impulsive, independent acts that have shaped her selfhood since early childhood. She realizes that her neurotic indecision, her coy "playing" at adultery, prevent her from achieving fulfillment: "Somewhere I had gone wrong; I had opened myself either too little or too much, I had not faced the choice that I should have faced and I had ended up with neither infidelity nor satisfaction" (p. 164).

Her sexual life thus becomes a sad comedy. When, finally, she does go to bed with Wyndham, in a ludicrous sickbed encounter, she "lets him get on with it" to fulfill the "debt" she feels she owes him – but "I wish to God that I could say that I enjoyed it" (p. 161). Then her unconscious masochistic wish for retribution is fulfilled when she is accidentally pinned against the garage wall by Wyndham's car as her husband comes home. Her affair with Wyndham is punctuated with accidents – the gas in the house, Flora's near drowning, then the ridiculous "consummation" scene where she is doubly trapped both by Wyndham's and his car's phallic force. She consciously reasons that the affair is unsuccessful because of the children – but, like everything else in her life, her attitude to them is riddled with contradictions. She tells us she is unresponsive sexually because she associates love-making with "babies. And being tired. And wanting to go to sleep. And I don't want that, I just want to have a good time" (p. 131), but also repeatedly insists that children have been an unexpected joy, and is glad when the affair is over and she can put her house in order.

For Emma, as for several of Drabble's women, children do root her in the world, giving her a stability that Julian, her male double, who shares her sexual ambivalence, does not have. Appropriately he commits suicide by drowning; the water imagery in the book is pervasive, imaging the annihilating implications of absolute human freedom.[49] Julian cannot cope with the messy realities of life: its necessary decisions, its sexual identities. And Emma knows all about him, for he is her childless, neurotic, freedom-seeking self: "Indecision drowned him. I used to be like Julian myself, but now I have two children, and you will not find me at the bottom of any river. I have grown into the earth. I am terrestrial" (p. 170). She proves "made for survival"; yet her strength is her rigidity. She realizes that she "would have to spend my life not in protecting myself but in protecting others from myself, starting with my

49

children" (p. 169). She accepts herself, but fatalistically accepts some disturbing traits: rigidity, compulsiveness, neurosis, frigidity, masochism.

Some readers view her as a pathological personality, while others find that her wit, candor, resilience and self-irony as a narrator woo them into a qualified acceptance.[50] Her rationalizations, compromises and accommodations in her role as wife, lover and mother, together with her longings for an identity that defies existing female models, evoke sympathy and identification even from readers who see Emma shaped and limited by social and cultural forces destructive of healthy female selfhood. Like other Drabble women, she too learns accommodation, to accept her imperfect self in an imperfect material and social world. This is vividly portrayed in the final scene, where she and David and the children enjoy an almost idyllic picnic ("Had David and I been two entirely different people, we might well that afternoon have been entirely happy; and even being what we were, we did not do too badly" (p. 172)). Then she discovers that one of the sheep they are admiring is being grabbed by a snake: "For the sake of the children," she pretends not to notice. Similarly for their sakes, she smoothes over the pathological aspects of her personality and the dissatisfactions in her life, and "gets on with" child-rearing. Romantic myth domesticated, *The Garrick Year* offers no resolution, no clear moral, though a clear moral awareness, presenting a complex character through her own sometimes candid and ironic, sometimes self-deceiving and self-justifying rhetoric. Drabble's narrative is so constructed that the reader must decide whether to accept or reject Emma's defenses, seeing them either as personally disturbed or disturbingly typical of the contemporary female condition.

*

Confident, efficient and independent, Rosamund Stacey of *The Millstone* (1965) finishes her degree, teaches, writes, and secures a university position while birthing and worrying about her illegitimate child Octavia, who has a congenitally

50

impaired heart. Her independence and resilience, her love for her child and growing assertion for the child's sake have aroused admiration in some readers;[51] others have concentrated upon the gaps in Rosamund's account of herself, seeing in her sexual reticence, her isolation, and her exclusive care of her child signs of a regressive "flight from womanhood."[52] As with Sarah and Emma, the inadequately explained gaps in Rosamund's narrative center on her inhibited sexuality and her diffident relationships with others. While she recognizes both as problems, she is, for an intelligent person, remarkably non-analytical and fatalistic: "There's nothing I can do about my nature, is there?" (M, p. 172), she rhetorically asks at the end of the book. In fact, a depressing degree of determinism colors her view: "a pattern forms before we are aware of it, and . . . what we think we make becomes a rigid prison making us" (p. 7).

While this attitude allows her to get on efficiently with her work, she, like Emma Evans, lives a significant part of her life as a studied lie, protecting her inner self. Dating two men who each think she is sleeping with the other, she conveniently avoids sexual and intimate relationships while preserving an *au courant* façade. Her sexual reticence stems not from moral prudery – indeed she feels she bears a shameful "A" for Abstinence rather than Adultery – but from "an apprehensive terror of the very idea of sex" (pp. 17–18). Unable to explain the cause of her terror, she can only accommodate herself to it. Not surprisingly, some readers cannot simply accept her ignorance and accommodation, and find clues to her condition in her relationship with her absent parents.

That Rosamund lives in her parents' flat with "the grand parental atmosphere which never quite left the place" (p. 25) is a graphic reminder that her life is largely defined and circumscribed by her parents' perceptions and values: a middle-class world with definite advantages, limitations, and "a well-established, traditional, English morality . . . it is my morality, whether I like it or not" (p. 121). Rosamund is acutely aware that the natural and middle-class advantages she inherits from her parents – their prestigiously located flat, her education, intelligence, good health and attractive appearance – create both special opportunities and liabilities: her sexual reticence, her isolation, her extreme diffidence and repression.

I am one reader who senses the repressed anger Rosamund directs toward her morally scupulous parents. They practice and have taught her "such tact, such withdrawal, such avoidance. Such fear of causing pain, such willingness to receive and take pains" (p. 145), that she cannot reach out openly to other people "in case I am not wanted. In case I am tedious" (p. 31). While she alludes to an unhappy childhood, she doesn't face her anger at this failure to bestow open and unconditional parental love, except for one telling allusion to *Washington Square*: "From another point of view, a more warm and fleshly point, they are perhaps as dangerous and cruel as that father in Washington Square" (p. 145). Her parents' characteristic self-denial and self-sacrifice have been duplicated by their daughter, so inhibiting her emotional responses to others that she is incapable of spontaneous love or friendship, or even of spontaneous dislike. Afraid of incurring a debt to others, or of being unfair, she scrupulously discharges any real or imagined debts or injustices. Part of her attitude also stems from her mother's valuing of female independence: "My mother, you know, was a great feminist. She brought me up to be equal. She made there be no question, no difference. I was equal. I am equal" (pp. 28–9). While such an upbringing undoubtedly spurs Rosamund's admirable career interests, "to be equal" seems to her mind to necessitate a denial of her femaleness as if it were a debility to be overcome. For example, when she ponders having her baby, she thinks: "it would serve me right, I thought, for having been born a woman in the first place. I couldn't pretend that I wasn't a woman, could I, however much I might try from day to day to avoid the issue?" (p. 16).

Her relationship with her novelist friend and flat-mate Lydia is a good example of the inhibiting dynamics of her relationships with others. Discovering that Lydia is using her as unflattering material in the novel she is writing, Rosamund, after the initial shock, is glad to learn that she "was still the donor," Lydia the "recipient," in their relationship. This denial of anger is duplicated later when through her "inadvertent" failure to close Lydia's door, her baby mangles and chews large segments of the manuscript. Only the baby, "this small living extension of myself" (p. 147), can display such spontaneous destructive urges. Rosamund, good child of her parents, translates them into "fair" and "just" self-sacrifice.

To be sure, the book turns largely on Rosamund's growing self-assertion as a result of the baby. She learns to insist upon her rights, even if it involves screaming hysterics as when she demands to see her baby in the hospital. She sees that this baby, far from being a millstone,[53] is a living and loving bond not only to another person, but to other people. She comes to see and appreciate the "human lot" around her, to experience the

> facts of inequality, of limitation, of separation, of the impossible, heart breaking uneven hardship of the human lot. I had always felt for others in theory and pitied the blows of fate and circumstance under which they suffered: but now, myself no longer free, myself suffering, I may say that I felt it in my heart. (p. 68)

Furthermore, she feels that forces larger than the self are operating through her pregnancy: "At times I had a vague and complicated sense that this pregnancy had been sent to me in order to reveal to me a scheme of things totally different from the scheme which I inhabited, totally removed from academic enthusiasms, social consciousness, etiolated undefined emotional connexions, and the exercise of free will" (p. 67). In fact, like many another of Drabble's characters, she feels herself to be on a Bunyanesque journey through a "moral landscape": "The geography of the locality took on . . . a fearful moral significance: it became a map of my weaknesses and my strengths, a landscape full of petty sloughs and pitfalls, like the one which Bunyan traversed" (p. 33).[54]

Yet Rosamund does not suddenly drop her defenses and reach out to others, as is clear from her anguish at the thought of imposing on her neighbors by asking them to watch the baby for a few minutes. In many ways she desires to establish with Octavia a cozy little world of two where Octavia's "uncritical love . . . left me free to bestow love. . . . Indeed, it must have been in expectation of this love that I insisted upon having her" (p. 115). I agree with Susan Spitzer that Rosamund's baby can be viewed as a fantasized replay of the loved and loving parent–child union of which she was deprived.[55]

That there is no room for a father for Octavia or a husband or lover for herself in this exclusive union is clear when Rosamund cannot traverse the "hopeless distance" (p. 172) between them by telling George of his inadvertent fatherhood, in spite of her poignant longings to do so. This is partly because she is afraid of incurring a debt to him, partly because of his own self-protective diffidence, which she sees that she formerly shared with him: "I neither envied nor pitied his indifference, for he was myself, the self that but for accident, but for fate, but for chance, but for womanhood, I would still have been" (p. 172) (a thought strikingly similar to Emma Evans's feelings about the male double who shares her ambivalent sexual identity, Julian). Furthermore, after Octavia's birth Rosamund has no revival of interest in men, although she thinks tenderly of George and listens to his safely disembodied voice on the radio. Gentle, diffident, possibly homosexual, George was the most de-sexed lover she could find to deflower and impregnate her with a cherished child-self, and now she scrupulously ejects him from the maternal nest.

While I am very likely overstating the unconscious motivations in her complex relationships with her lover, her child and her parents, Rosamund none the less surely speaks only one part of the truth, the conscious, rational, articulate part. Because this novel has provoked radically different opinions of Rosamund, some readers, Ellen Cronan Rose and Susan Spitzer in particular, have puzzled over the problem of "distance" between narrator and author. Margaret Drabble honestly admits that she quite often does not have analytical distance from her characters:

I don't understand them. I wait and see what they do. I don't feel superior because I'm sort of mystified; I present them with certain problems, which is the plot; the plot is the problem they're presented with, then they have to resolve it, and quite often I don't know whether I admire them or go along with them, or think they should have tried harder, I just don't know. As one doesn't know when a friend makes a decision; you don't know whether she should have left him or she should have had the baby; you don't know.[56]

Drabble looks at her books as explorations not declamations of the "truth." While it is difficult to say, then, "to what extent Margaret Drabble has expressed Rosamund Stacey's unconscious *consciously*,"[57] the characterization is none the less suggestive, convincing and compelling. Drabble's novels are such that the reader, rather than the author, tries to effect closure. As human beings are viewed differently by different people, so Drabble's first-person narrators create different impressions on different readers; her narratives lie open to multiple, divergent, and inconclusive views.

*

In *The Waterfall* (1969) the multiple, divergent and inconclusive interpretations reside in the narration itself, which alternates between third- and first-person points of view because the narrator, Jane Gray, cannot sustain the hypotheses she constructs without interrupting to lament the gaps, the omissions, which each version conceals. "Lies, lies, it's all lies. A pack of lies" (W, p. 84). The novel centers on the love affair between Jane Gray and her cousin Lucy's husband James. Deserted by her husband, closed up within her house, withdrawing into an overheated room in which she is about to deliver a baby, Jane Gray has reached a pathological state of passivity and agoraphobia. Into this dry, empty house and life come both a new baby and a new lover. The novel records Jane's ambivalent and conflict-ridden view of this affair — which on one hand seems to be both sexually and emotionally liberating, and on the other to be an immoral, trivial fantasy with disturbing and largely unexamined psychological implications.

This novel is the technically sophisticated culmination of Drabble's earlier first-person narratives, for the skeptical "I" of *The Waterfall* can be seen as a dissenting "reader's response," a role generated by the "gaps" in these earlier novels but not "written into" them. The unwritten and unexplained gaps in the earlier narrators' presentation of themselves give those novels their hidden complexity, generate considerable psychological resonance, and draw readers into a participatory role. Now *The Waterfall* disarmingly incorporates the reader's skeptical voice – Jane "reads" and criticizes her own "story" – though that voice may not completely satisfy readers, nor coincide necessarily with their views.

Breaking the illusion of the story, the first-person narrator confesses about fifty pages into the text: "It won't, of course, do: as an account, I mean, of what took place" (p. 46). Jane claims to have cast her experience into a "fictitious form: adding a little here, abstracting a little there," attempting to "reconstitute it in a form" she "can accept," trying "to understand what I am doing" even if it means inventing "a morality that condones me" (pp. 52–3). Alternating between first and third person, Jane swings from lyrical romanticism to caustic cynicism, often undercutting within a few sentences, as well as repudiating chapters, the elaborate metaphors she has just spun, the explanations she has just offered.

The first-person explications are themselves, of course, self-justifying versions of the "real" and the "true." While the tremendous anger Jane directs at her parents, for example, is unequivocally presented, Jane's self-pitying condemnation may invite further conjecture. Jane is angry about her mother's preference for her sister and unconscious rejection of herself at birth, and about the confusion engendered by her parents' duplicity, hypocrisy, class-consciousness, and denial. She claims that as a child "I felt all the time afraid that any word of mine, any movement, my mere existence, might shatter them all into fragments" (pp. 51–2). Jane does not isolate, however, what seems to be a naive, narcissistic belief that the world and other people are profoundly affected by herself, that she can indeed "shatter" others into bits with a "look."

Carrying her childhood denial and evasion of feelings into adulthood, Jane claims she married Malcolm because he had seemed "a safe dependable reliable man to go around with" (p. 91), a man who would make her "a different, better, safer person." Later when, ironically, this seemingly "safe" effeminate husband beats her head against the bedroom wall and finally deserts her, she prefers to take the blame upon herself, claiming that she drove him out by her "dreariness, apathy, and misery," by "my bad housekeeping, by my staring at the wall, by my too evident frigidity" (p. 110). But in the masochism too eagerly taken on readers may again find Jane's readiness to see another's behavior as governed by herself. She blinds herself to what she later suspects but still cannot quite put into words, that perhaps Malcolm is a homosexual.

Where Jane appears most imperceptive is in her account of her relationship with her cousin Lucy. So near in age, so like her physically and emotionally, Lucy was, she claims, "my sister, my fate, my example: her effect on me was incalculable" (p. 114). Jane sees herself getting married because Lucy got married, having children because Lucy had children, and carefully scrutinizing Lucy's house for "the secret of matrimony, the secret key to being a woman, and living with a man" (p. 128). She tries to deny what she further suspects: "It couldn't be possible that I wanted James because he was hers, because I wanted to be her. It wasn't so, it wasn't so" (p. 130). Locked into an excessively polite deference, Jane must indeed study her cousin's *house* for clues about her marriage and her life, for she cannot talk with Lucy about them. When after the accident Lucy registers at the hotel as "Jane Gray" because Jane has already registered as "Lucy Otford," Jane and Lucy speculate that the affair must have had "something to do" with their relationship with one another, but Jane is reluctant to think about it. Readers will feel compelled, I believe, to try to explain her reluctance.

I think, for example, that in some ways Lucy functions as the mother that Jane's mother failed to be, but only in being a desirable image of female selfhood, not in providing nurturing acceptance and love. Rather, Lucy is, as Jane recognizes, a "schizoid double" (p. 210). Where Jane frigidly closes her body and opts out of the "game of sexual selection," finding it the "most savage" game in the world (p. 124), Lucy plays it vicariously for her. Lucy's literal and figurative "open door" at university results in a trail of broken hearts, and she ends up with the game's prize, a sexually attractive husband. So, on the one hand, the incestuous union of Jane–James–Lucy may be a symbiotic attempt to incorporate Lucy – Jane's schizoid double, her chosen "mother" – into herself through James. On the other, it may be an attempt to triumph over and hurt this rival self, this alter ego, this diffident, unloving "mother."

The abundant birth imagery surrounding the affair will undoubtedly suggest to many post-Freud (and post-Norman Holland[58]) readers what Jane, even in her most sardonic mood, does not quite spell out, that she and James indulge in an oral fantasy in which *James* is the loving mother and she the helpless infant who is tied absolutely to his solicitous care. Jane claims to be "in bondage," with a "total lack of volition," devoting "her life to this preoccupation. It sucked, obsessively, all other interests from her . . . her body was remembering him, it was fainting and opening for each word, each touch, each gesture, each one relived a hundred times" (p. 135). While she claims that "it was worse, it was worse than I can ever say" (p. 164), readers may feel that it is pretty bad as she tells it and may wonder about the kind of mother she is being to her own children while she herself is playing the infant.

While Jane perhaps does not see the extent to which her affair is a regressive fantasy, she does know only too well that it is a romantic one, nurtured and built upon fictional prototypes. Jane's "fiction" is acted out against a rich backdrop of culturally shared "womenslore." Indeed, it is a very self-indulgent re-enactment of that perennial female fantasy, Sleeping Beauty's awakening by Prince Charming — with some modern-day emendations. This Sleeping Beauty lies all alone, passive and withdrawn, exhausted and abandoned, with unwashed hair in a bloody, "disgusting" childbirth bed, when she is unexpectedly cared for and found overwhelmingly beautiful and desirable by a very attractive, dangerous-looking, but really remarkably gentle man, a man who is neither her husband nor the father of the baby, but much more erotically, her cousin's husband. This undemanding lover waits patiently and idly, solicitously holding her hand in "chaste incestuous desire" during her post-partum recovery to "awaken" her finally, not through a kiss, but through sexual orgasm: "Her own voice, in that strange sobbing cry of rebirth. A woman delivered. She was his offspring, as he, lying there between her legs, had been hers" (p. 151). Not only does this beauty have adulterous, incestuous sex and live to tell about it – and so eludes the sad sisterhood of hundreds of literary precursors who learn too late that the wages of erotic indulgence are death – she is miraculously restored through the "amazing fate" of her "sexual salvation."

But Jane's ringing affirmation is balanced by skepticism, belittlement and doubt. Fearing that her life is imitating fiction, Jane disdainfully proclaims that their affair is "some ridiculous imitation of a fictitious passion" (p. 202). They delicately construct this "islanded world" (p. 75) "walled . . . in like invisible glass" (p. 136) from the "dangerous wastes" (p. 44) around them. Jane is perplexed by fictions and fantasies that are "real," and by reality that is "unreal" and non-essential in her own life and in the lives of others:

Which was Charlotte Brontë's man, the one she created and wept for and longed for, or the poor curate that had her and killed her, her sexual measure, her sexual match? I had James, oh God, I had him, but I can't describe the condition of that possession; the world that I lived in with him – the dusty Victorian house, the fast car, the race tracks, the garages, the wide bed – it was a foreign country to me, some Brussels of the mind. (p. 84)

Jane struggles to accept the apparent paradox that within this elaborate fantasy she experiences the first real emotional and sexual communion of her life. The climax of the experience, her first sexual orgasm, is a metaphoric waterfall, in which she falls "drenched and drowned, down there at last in the water not high in her lonely place" (p. 150). Jane is aware that there is something embarrassing and slightly ridiculous about placing such ponderous significance upon what is, from some perspectives, ineffable and trivial. Similarly, readers are likely to be as puzzled as Jane. Should we view this cascading waterfall as the watery equivalent of the Lawrentian "baptism of fire in passion," an initiation into adult sexuality and fully achieved selfhood? Or are we suspicious about all this oceanic and birth imagery, which we may read as indicative of the pre-eminence of the oral fantasy in which James and Jane alternately play the maternal role: "She was his offspring, as he, lying there between her legs, had been hers." Readers may also find Jane's inflated, hyperbolic language suspicious and may wonder whether it verges on self-parody, or if it further evidences a narcissistic world view. Her affair is a preordained "miracle," an "amazing fate," which "saves" her, embodying or perhaps altering her "destiny." Jane's actions or inactions, she suspects, have significance on a cosmic scale. Even the accident is a vehicle of her cosmic destiny, punishing her for immoral behavior, completing her rebirth and delivering her into the "real" world.

Moreover, Jane carefully edits her story for readers. She maintains a self-protective distance, by reminding us that her "fiction" may or may not bear a direct relationship to the "facts." She says, for example, that because she cannot find an inherent coherence in her experience she is tempted to impose one. She undermines readers' apprehension of events narrated earlier by admitting near the end of the novel that she "deliber-

60

ately exaggerated my helplessness, my dislocation, as a plea for clemency" (p. 226). She playfully and disarmingly discusses other ways she could have ended the novel:

> Perhaps I should have killed James in the car, and that would have made a neat, a possible ending. . . . Or, I could have maimed James so badly, in this narrative, that I would have been allowed to have him, as Jane Eyre had her blinded Rochester. But I hadn't the heart to do it, I loved him too much, and anyway it wouldn't have been the truth because the truth is that he recovered. (p. 231)

Jane also admits to toying with the idea of ending the narrative with James's impotence, "the little, twentieth-century death" (p. 238) – an ironic modern inversion of the "little death" of Renaissance literature, sexual orgasm – but she opts instead for a "feminine ending," which, like the poetic one, is irresolute, inconclusive.

Indeed, remission from the heavily orchestrated endings of women's stories, lives and books is exactly what her story – with its other kind of "feminine ending" – enacts, and it is here where modern perspectives are interjected into a traditional female predicament. Jane, in a sense, has her cake and eats it too – engaging in a self-indulgent fantasy without being locked finally into a fantasy world, enjoying erotic fulfillment without paying the usual price. "One shouldn't get away with such things" (p. 232), Jane thinks, as she recalls doubles who do not: Maggie Tulliver, who "never slept with her man: she did all the damage there was to be done, to Lucy, to herself, to the two men who loved her, and then like a woman of another age, she refrained" (p. 153); Jane Eyre, who got her man only after he was, in effect, unmanned; Lady Jane Grey, her namesake, who paid for her nine-day queenly glory with her beheading. Rather, in Jane's living of the perennial romantic story, the ending is different: it eludes narrative closure and "morality," excludes the "ever after" of both fantasy and tragedy. Jane's prince does one day come and awaken her sleeping self, but the lovers do not marry and live happily every after. Nor do they cleanly break off. Rather, after the accident Jane and James continue to see each other when they can. Their affair "lingers on." Jane laments, "it isn't artistic. . . . It isn't moral either" (p. 232). Moreover, Jane neither "refrains" from sexual indulgence like Maggie, nor "pays" for it with her death like so many heroines before her. The "feminine ending" of her volume includes an ironic postscript, however, in which Jane notes that the woman does still continue to pay, just as in the old days, only now the price is not so starkly dramatic. The ingloriously "grey" price this latter-day Jane pays for her "sexual salvation" is "thrombosis or neurosis: one can take one's pick" (p. 239), for had she not stopped taking birth-control pills after the accident, she might have died of a thrombotic clot.

Yet I think Jane has learned to live with such indelicate ironies, paradoxes and disharmonies; she, like other Drabble characters, learns accommodation. She is able by the end of the novel to carry on contentedly with her life as she could not before: cleaning her house, nurturing her children, visiting her in-laws, writing and publishing poetry, talking with her literary friends, seeing James occasionally, expecting to see Malcolm sometime. Typically Drabblesque, Jane's unresolved and ambivalent position "is all so different from what I had expected. It is all so much more cheerful" (p. 234). Jane's cheerful acceptance is an uneasy yoking of the search for free feeling with a measure of control, of sexual radicalism with a desire for moral and social stability. Like the Goredale Scar, the waterfall Jane and James visit near the end the book, Jane's sexual "liberation" is carefully circumscribed, "a wildness contained in a bodily limit" (p. 236).

I can understand, however, why some readers may be uneasy with this compromise. Jane has shown a distinct reluctance to make some unflattering connections and observations. She doesn't really know or want to know Lucy, even though she has modelled her life upon her cousin's. She doesn't see her children as people with their own separate needs and problems. One suspects that she doesn't know the first thing about her husband, including his sexual preference. She does not want to know anything about James outside the fantasy life they built together. Most importantly, she does not truly see herself, or want anyone else to do so. Although she claims that James "saw" her as she had never been seen before, what does he see? The beautiful, helpless woman of his "carefully edited" sexual fantasy, not the intelligent, complex, disturbed woman readers come to know. While Jane retreats from closeness to readers too, playfully hiding behind the multiple layers of fictionalizing in the novel, it is a credit to Margaret Drabble's skill as a novelist that she creates a character with such credibility, such psychological resonance, that readers may feel that they know more about Jane than she does herself, more than Jane, in fact, wants us to "see."[59]

In Jane Gray, Drabble has given us a familiar literary type, an unreliable narrator; but more than this, the novel profoundly questions the very stability of character and the ability to know one's self and the world with any degree of certainty. Jane has discovered intuitively what post-structuralists have postulated, that reality is necessarily mediated through language and that different "codes" create different discourses. She is confronted with the evidence that "the ways of regarding an event, so different, don't add up to a whole; they are mutually exclusive: the social view, the sexual view, the circumstantial view, the moral view, these visions contradict each other; they do not supplement one another, they cancel one another, they destroy one another. They cannot co-exist" (p. 46). Traditional liberal morality and traditional realistic fiction are both shaken by this observation. Even though Jane Gray (and Margaret Drabble) sees her life within the context of a tradition of literary and real heroines who precede her, her story is finally fundamentally different: the old patterns are broken, however nostalgically one may look back to the old epistemological and moral certainties – and the female limitations – they embodied. If, as A. S. Byatt has cogently postulated, British novelists of the 1960s and 1970s display "an awareness of the difficulty of 'realism' combined with a strong moral attachment to its values, a formal need to comment on their fictiveness combined with a strong sense of the value of a habitable imagined world, a sense that models, literature and 'the tradition' are ambiguous and problematic goods combined with a profound nostalgia for, rather than rejection of, the great works of the past,"[60] then *The Waterfall* is a very typical book of its times with affinities to the other works Byatt cites: Iris Murdoch's *The Black Prince* (1973), Angus Wilson's *As If by Magic* (1973), and Doris Lessing's *The Golden Notebook* (1962). I would also add John Fowles's *The French Lieutenant's Woman* (1969) to this list, which Malcolm Bradbury has called "an exemplary book of the 1960s" for its attempt "to reconcile a modern, self-sceptical, post-existential modern text with a traditional one."[61] *The Waterfall* too attempts this reconciliation, and both novels end with post-modernist irresolution which draws readers into active engagement with the text.

3

GOLDEN REALMS

While *The Waterfall* records Jane Gray's equivocal breaking out from the isolation of her own mind and body, the third-person novels of Drabble's middle period – *Jerusalem the Golden* (1967), *The Needle's Eye* (1972) and *The Realms of Gold* (1975) – move yet further away from the solipsistic spaces of the earliest novels. (Although *Jerusalem the Golden* was written before *The Waterfall*, I have taken the liberty of arranging Drabble's novels in what I see as natural groupings.) They explore a more graphic exodus from the constricting world of childhood: its geography, class-bound values, moral outlook. Northern landscapes are rejected in each of these novels for the cosmopolitan environment of London; the characters "by will and by strain" eject themselves from oppressive childhoods and create new selves and new worlds out of preconceived "golden" fantasies, be they literary, religious, or archaeological in origin: a golden Jerusalem, a Bunyanesque holy city, realms of gold. Yet can one really escape the past and create oneself anew? "It's terribly hard to break away from a background," Margaret Drabble muses; "our own family has been rather prone to it . . . family separation . . . or what is the word, diffusion, . . . happens a great deal in our family, and I think in most English, lower-middle-class families, and I do think that it is important to know where you come from, and to reconcile yourself to the bits you don't like. To know one's self, to know all that is behind one."[62] The conflicting needs to break away from the past and to come to terms with it inform these three novels and recall others by Drabble's contemporaries, such as Lessing's Martha Quest series (1952–69), Braine's *Room at the Top* (1957), and Fowles's *The French Lieutenant's Woman* (1969).

From *Jerusalem the Golden* to *The Needle's Eye* and *The Realms of Gold*, one can trace Drabble's skillful and increasingly playful use of the third-person point of view and her gradual broadening of novelistic space. The single central character of Clara Maugham in *Jerusalem the Golden* is replaced in *The Needle's Eye* by dual central characters, Rose Vassiliou and Simon Camish (Drabble's first male protagonist); in *The Realms of Gold*, a host of characters are drawn and "orchestrated" by an omniscient narrator. Literary influence continues to shape Drabble's work. *Jerusalem the Golden* was, she admits in her Bennett biography, "profoundly affected" by Bennett and by his character Hilda Lessways, and indeed by his Naturalist methods and concerns. *The Needle's Eye*, modelled on James's *The Portrait of a Lady*,[63] is characterized by its skillful adaptation of Jamesian central intelligence and its probing psychological and moral complexities. The narration of *The Realms of Gold* recalls that of Fielding and Thackeray; its interconnected network of characters, images, levels of reference, and literary allusions (including Woolf, Shakespeare, Milton, Wordsworth, Updike, Stendhal, and others[64]) initiates Drabble's later style.

In these novels Drabble can well seem to be linking her work to the neo-realistic tradition of the English novel, rejecting the experimental method of *The Waterfall* and the subjective concerns of her earliest books for omnisciently narrated fictions ordered by coincidental plot, dominated by character, and infused with social concerns of class, custom and morality. Yet while these novels do, in fact, link up to that tradition, they still continue to be in many ways double-voiced and equivocal, mediating between traditional humanistic realism and modern perspectives. "Omniscience has its limits," the narrator of *The Realms of Gold* candidly admits, calling attention to the fictionality of this carefully constructed world. Similarly character is not at all stable, and perhaps not knowable. Because the characters' lives are such a composite of psychological determinism and willful self-creation, the boundaries between the real and the imagined are equivocal for character and reader alike. Furthermore, Drabble's use of houses and landscapes, real and metaphorical, as objective correlatives of mental states lend considerable subtlety and depth to these novels, dramatizing the intense preoccupation Drabble shares with the Romantics with the "effect of landscape upon the soul." Despite the complex modern perspectives Drabble brings to her narratives, she is resolutely traditional in her liberal belief that the individual must link up to something larger than the self – a place, a community, shared values, the past. The generating tension of these middle novels resides in the apparent freedom of the individual to create a new self coupled with his or her necessary circumscription within geographical, communal, and historical contexts.

*

Jerusalem the Golden (1967) does indeed seem different from the other early novels because it is told in the third person, though the most interesting and problematic aspect of the book remains its point of view. The narrator's attitude to Clara Maugham is infused with such a delicate mixture of sympathy and judgment, the familiar open-endedness, that the reader is once more tempted to supply the balance and effect the resolution. Clara's story is trite enough – that of the naive provincial girl with good looks, brains, cunning and sexual opportunism who propels herself into the sophisticated world of her dreams. But where in slick fiction readers are allowed to rest comfortably in an unequivocal relation to the central character, here they are not, being pushed into an uneasy mixture of sympathy for and condemnation of Clara's determination to escape. Like *The Needle's Eye* and *The Realms of Gold* to follow, *Jerusalem the Golden* has a vivid concreteness and imagistic density which, palpably, subtly and artfully, embodies its moral complexity. Clara's search for life and survival takes her across a familiar British landscape, from northern toughness and barrenness to a more open but more ambiguous world. It is a familiar enough mapping of the English social and moral landscape, treated with a realism, and a common-sense understanding of the need for it, which had not till now become a recognizable part of Drabble's tone. Yet the possibility that the real is a mode of imprisonment is part of Clara's revolt; she longs for a world of larger imagination, more than real – the "terrestrial paradise" embodied in the title.

Once again, the textured quality of the book comes from the way houses are made intimately revealing of the lives of their inhabitants. Clara's mother's house – in suburban Northam, the northern industrial town Drabble also uses elsewhere – is for Clara more than a place of habitation; it is infused with all she chooses to reject and escape, and becomes a hated example of a life devoid of sentiment, warmth, honesty and openness, with each item in it a manifestation of the attitudes and opinions of her joyless mother. The table, for example, witnesses to "so many foibles, so many fixed and rigid rules," like the use of plastic mats but not a plastic table cloth, because "plastic table cloths were the last resort of the working classes"; the slop basin is a "symbol of the traditionally correct" which Clara finds "always painfully conspicuous, an indictment of a way of life," and affects her like "some shameful family secret" (*JG*, pp. 44–5). The "cramped sitting room" emblemizes claustrophobic family and social life; "Nobody ever visited their house except through obligations, and such family celebrations as still persisted had been transformed into grim duties" (p. 55). By the end of the book, Clara frees herself from this oppressive setting. At first she doubts her escape; when her mother becomes seriously ill after Clara has invented just such an illness as cover for a meeting in Paris with her lover Gabriel, she fears the "iron fingers which she had tried, so wilfully, so desperately to elude; a whole system was after her, and she the final victim, the last sacrifice, the shuddering product merely of her past" (p. 191). And yet when alone in the house she finds she has over-reacted: "What immense folly had ever made her fear such a fate? It was nearly over; the house was about to expire, it would be taken to pieces and there would be nothing left of it" (p. 194).

But what kind of survivor is Clara? And at what cost? Can one throw off the past, break the laws of determinism, construct oneself anew? It is here that, again, the provocative gaps arise in the space between Clara's perceptions of herself, and ours of her. When young, she has seen her life as a tragically impoverished plant, seeking to grow in Northam's cold, barren soil. Later, "she had to concede that she must have fallen happily upon some dry sandy fissure, where a few grains of sand, a few drops of moisture, had been enough to support her trembling and tenacious life. Because she would live, she would survive" (p. 26). The possibility of living, not meanly like her mother, but in luxurious growth, seems sanctioned by a parable about two weeds growing on a river bank – "one of them conserved its energy, and grew low and small and brown, with its sights set on a long life, while the other put forth all its strength into growing tall and into colouring itself a beautiful green" (p. 34). Picked up by a beautiful girl, the tall weed blushes and dies content; the short laughs and lives until next year. It is the "moral ambivalence" of the tale that draws Clara:

> Incredibly enough it seemed to end with a choice. It would hardly have been possible for it to support beauty and extravagance and pleasure at the expense of mere survival, but it did at least hint that such a view could be held, and its mere admission of this possibility was to Clara profoundly satisfying. (pp. 34–5)

It is the "moral ambivalence" of the tale that is duplicated for the reader in the life of "beauty and extravagance and pleasure" Clara constructs for herself. And she indeed "constructs" herself; she "had no confidence that time would bring with it inevitable growth: she grew by will and by strain" (p. 26). In an energy of social survival she uses her assets – her intelligence, her breasts, her boyfriends – as a means to an end, getting out

69

of Northam. Once an oddity and handicap, her intelligence facilitates her escape, getting her on school-trips to Paris to practice her French, then to London on a scholarship. Her looks, which she had assumed to be ordinary, blossom into full-breasted glory and win her a place in the smart set at school: "She was naturally gratified by this change of front, and drew the appropriate moral – the possession of big breasts, like the possession of a tendency to acquire good examination results, implies power" (p. 46). Her boyfriends, too, are chosen for their ability to offer links with and awareness of "other worlds" and their usefulness; she discards Walter Ash when she has to lead him past a herd of cows, thinking "this isn't good enough for me, I shall get further if I'm pulled, I can't waste time in going first" (p. 29). Her eagerness to slough off the past and enter a new world is so amusingly told that we can surely identify with her youthful search for sophistication. But we become increasingly uneasy about the toll the will and strain takes, and the kind of person she attempts to create.

Yet the world she seeks has an imaginative power set against hard realism: "The world of the figurative was Clara's world of refuge. The literal world which she inhabited was so plainly hostile that she seized with ardour upon any references to any other mode of being" (p. 32). She is particularly impressed by the hymn "Jerusalem the Golden" because she pictures not a heavenly but "some truly terrestrial paradise, where beautiful people in beautiful houses spoke of beautiful things" (p. 32). Meeting the Denhams, she cannot distinguish between fantasy and realism. They are totally in keeping with her earthly dream. Theirs is a contrasting house, a lesson in graceful, comfortable, elegant living; it vindicates the "aristocratic ideal" (p. 97), and Clelia's room, with its "profusion of the most diverse and wonderful objects" (p. 91), amazes and delights her, especially with its

> sense of prolonged nursery associations. The childhood objects were not only lovely in themselves, they were a link with some past and pleasantly remembered time, a time not

violently shrugged off and rejected, but a time to be lived with, in happy recollection, a time which could well bear remembering. (p. 92)

But where Clelia's room can link with the past, Clara's barren room at university displays deliberate severance: she makes no attempt "to decorate it, to domesticate it, to possess it" (p. 81). She keeps it, like her mind, an empty space in which to build, "by will and by strain," a new self, now modelled on the Denhams, whose mental world, too, is densely crowded with concepts and conversation, emotions and intimacy. After the choking silence of her mother's house, their surfeit affects her like rich "strange food," and "her mind stretched and cracked in an effort to take them in" (pp. 106–7), to a point where on one occasion she throws up.

Clara's refusal of her own past indeed makes Clelia her desired double, and she unquestionably gets involved with Clelia's brother Gabriel in part because he so strongly resembles his sister; like Jane Gray in *The Waterfall*, she "introjects" another woman's identity by sexually taking over her man. That the man is not the husband but the cherished married brother gives, as both Clara and Gabriel see, an incestuous aura to the union. But Clara sees no harm in this, and Gabriel, so perfectly in keeping with her golden fantasies, seems, as his name suggests, an angel, a "superior creature" fallen from "paradise" (p. 115). There are clear enough indications that his life is far from heavenly (again shown most vividly through a house, Gabriel's and his wife's, which is depressingly ramshackle and lacks the elegance and integration of his parents'), but Clara chooses not to think about it, or know everything about him: "She liked the unknown, she likes to feel familiar with the unknown" (p. 155). Privy to more information (Gabriel's thoughts are summarized in parts of chapter 8), the reader must temper Clara's idealized view of Gabriel with what she chooses to ignore: his domestic and professional worries and frustrations, his wife Phillipa's acute depression. While Clara sleeps deeply and well on their Paris visit, "he could not sleep: he lay there restless, thinking of his wife, of his children, of his bank balance, and wondering to himself, irritably, sadly, why he had not arranged to have his car serviced while he was away" (p. 168).

That much of Clara's "success" is based on keeping other and harder facts unknown is the essence of the story. The pattern has been set by the "stony frontage" Mrs Maugham has constructed emotionally between herself and her daughter. But Clara sustains the obstruction, preferring to look at nothing which can help her understand or have sympathy for her mother – for example, the barren Christmases of her mother's childhood, which she replicates: "when, occasionally, she [Clara] glimpsed some faint light of causation, she recoiled from it and shut her eyes in horror, preferring the darkness to such bitter illumination" (p. 55). Even when she belatedly discovers her own "place of birth" in her mother's girlhood notes, poetry and dreams of escape, and sees their kinship, she does not communicate the discovery to her dying mother, and is just the more grateful for her own escape. As her mother dies, Clara sees "with relief" that "there would be nothing, that she would not be called upon to give, that she could merely answer meanness with meanness" (p. 200).

Mrs Maugham's fierce unloving reserve makes her perhaps the worst of the many oppressive mothers in Drabble's fiction,[65] and one can surely sympathize with Clara's reciprocal meanness. Yet, as she herself suspects earlier, "perhaps a better daughter might have found a way to soften such a mother" (p. 58). Clara will not retract the psychological "miles" she and her mother have put between themselves, and in thus choosing not to give, not to forgive, not to understand, not to know, she gets out of her mother's house. But ironically she takes with her the quality in her mother she finds most abhorrent, the inability to love: "'I am all nerve, I am hard, there is no love in me, I am too full of will to love' . . . love, desperately, eluded her; she had not been taught to love, she had lacked those expensive, private lessons" (p. 165). I think we would feel more sympathy for Clara if she were more consistently concerned about her emotional barrenness.

Rather, Clara is for the most part pleased with herself and her life. She develops a rigid tensile strength, but she chooses a disturbingly superficial, empty, and unconnected world. So much energy has gone into escaping that "she did not know what she wanted"; she felt "the bitter limits of her own hitherto illimitable designs" (p. 169). Her designs dealt primarily with appearing to be different from what she was, for model herself on Clelia as she will, she cannot "become" Clelia; she cannot duplicate her warmth, her depth, her talent, her loving connectedness to others, her fortunate and happy rootedness within a mind and body, house and geography, family and history, time and place. So Clara chooses to polish appearances, to forgo substance, and to resist connection. When Gabriel calls her at her mother's house she agrees to a resumption of their affair with a journey back from Northam with him, because she is enchanted by "all the years of future tender intrigue, a tender blurred world where Clelia and Gabriel and she herself in shifting and ideal conjunctions met and drifted and met once more like the constellations in the heavens: a bright and peopled world, thick with starry inhabitants, where there was no ending, no parting, but an eternal vast incessant rearrangement" (pp. 205–6).

Perhaps because Gabriel insists upon seeing the house, Clara will begin to accept rather than deny the large part of herself bound to it, but more likely she will not. At any rate her future is left open. The novel remains open to varying judgments of Clara,[66] but I view it as an incisive illustration of Drabble's belief that "we are not free from our past, we are never free of the claims of others, and we ought not wish to be."[67] In pretending to be free from the past, from the claims of others, and from the human community, in pretending to live a golden fantasy, Clara is indeed displaying "a very inadequate way of looking at life." She had better, as she suspects, "reserve her gratitude" for escape from her mother's house "until more safe and later days" (p. 196).

*

The Needle's Eye (1972) gives us a much more sophisticated and complex examination of the issue central to *Jerusalem the Golden*: can one cut oneself off from the past and make oneself anew? It is developed with more characters and in dense moral, social, and psychological contexts. In this novel Drabble's omniscient narration is seemingly trustworthy, thorough, and conventional. Yet if in the traditional realistic novel we are accustomed to finding an implicit set of values against which the characters are drawn and measured, then this apparently traditional work subverts these expectations, by demonstrating that it is "impossible, really, to make one's mind up about any other human person, even one's own children whose whole life has unrolled before one's eyes, whose every influence is known: they were so contradictory, so inconstant, so confusing a mass of shifting characteristics" (*NE*, p. 156). With Jamesian density, the novel is built upon the recollections and reflections of Simon and Rose, who have each constructed a life set in opposition to their childhood worlds. The movements of each up and down the social scale intersect and counterpoint those of the other. Simon, a successful lawyer with a wealthy wife, a fashionable house, and upper-middle-class friends, has cut himself off from his northern working-class background. Rose has rejected first her parents and their wealth and later her husband Christopher to live with her three children in a working-class district.

Simon's attempt to make himself afresh appears on the surface to be successful, but he suffers an extreme degree of alienation from others, from his environment, and from his own emotions. While admiring the "comfortable bourgeois texture" of the flat of his friends Nick and Diana, Simon himself cannot be comfortable amid such acquired "texture" either in his friends' house or within his own. Still appalled by the opulence of his new world and the way his friends take it for granted, he is overcome with hate for them because "they were not his and he could not have them" (p. 18). Full of self-contempt and feeling forever alien to the upper-middle-class

74

life he has made for himself, he damningly recollects his "cold, overwrought, conscience-stricken, guilt-ridden childhood" (p. 65), his mother's unlovely ambition and sacrifice, the living on will which his drive to success necessitated, and the devastating toll it has exacted in his emotional life. Like his mother, Simon is repelled by the ostentatious vulgarities of his wife Julie and her family, even as he is drawn fatally to them: "There was in Julie a coarseness and a lack of discrimination that must have attracted him to her, as one is attracted, compelled, to approach one's own doom, to live out one's own hereditary destiny" (p. 70). Moreover, he feels that "his whole life – the clothes he wore, the car he drove, the way he spoke, the house he lived in – was an act of misrepresentation" (p. 138); it seems to him to embody "an eternal human pattern of corruption." He feels that their lifestyle is artificial and unnatural, that "he and Julie had over-reached themselves, they had set their sights too high, and therefore it was that they clashed and bled, and that their faces were lined with the furrows of an unsuitable strain" (p. 187), that a house such as theirs, built upon sand, will not stand. The severity of his self-contempt and moral disgust with his life recalls Wilson's powerful portrait of George Middleton in *Anglo-Saxon Attitudes* (1956).

Having "grown up amidst too much physical intimacy – houses too small, settees too narrow, bedrooms too full," Simon has sought to find for himself a "clear, empty space" only to discover that "the world of touch would be lost forever" (pp. 54–5). While moving through the new affluent environment, then, he feels "dry, dry as a bone" (p. 19). Simon's emotional barrenness, he feels, has been precipitated in part by his compulsive and driving "sense of obligation," which has sapped even his zest for life (p. 113). Because of this "sense of obligation" he married his wife Julie when he no longer "felt" like marrying her, and because of it he stays with her, despite the desperate unhappiness, the vicious ill will, and the caustic and cruel exchanges between them.

Responding to a critic, Drabble has suggested that the reader must not take Simon's underrating of himself as objectively valid. Emphasizing his positive actions, his responsibility for others, his idealism, his "effort towards justice" in his role as a lawyer, she characterizes him as a man who strives for the good.[68] Be that as it may, he is also a man who feels hopelessly shaped and maimed by a hereditary and environmental conditioning inimical to personal wholeness and integrity (he believes in fact that "people endure not one lifetime but many, layers and layers of evolved suffering handed down, worse than anything Freud had ever proposed in the way of predestination" (p. 30)), a man unable to reach out to others, a man shockingly cut off from his own children, a man who is finally resigned to passive endurance of the unsatisfactory life he has made for himself. Simon's sensitivity, intelligence and probing self-examination stand aside his low self-esteem, his emotional barrenness, his passive acquiescence. Like so many of Drabble's characters, he lacks psychic integration, although he, like they, is often capable of efficiently functioning in a relatively cheerful manner. Is this all one can expect from life? Is he realistically accepting his responsibilities, recognizing the common-sense limits, and playing his "proper part" in the human community, as Drabble suggests in her comment upon the book; or is his decision to remain with Julie, like Rose's to return to Christopher, an example of his tragic and defeatist "yearning for self sacrifice," as one critic has claimed?[69] I shall return to this key critical issue after looking at Rose's complementary role in the novel.

Rose is harder to assess, in part because she is seen largely through Simon's loving and sympathetic eyes. The tension between admirable acceptance of obligation and pathological self-denial is intensified in Rose's several flamboyant gestures of renunciation, self-assertion, and self-denial. Similarly reacting against an unhappy childhood, Rose also attempts to create willfully a new self and a new world: "All alone . . . I arrest the course of nature" (p. 117), though her whole effort is to repudiate instead of to acquire the class advantages that lure Simon into an alien world. However, Rose's radical gestures of repudiation are based on some rather absurd and simplistic notions, generated by her strange childhood nurse, Noreen, a religious fanatic who has ranted about the evils of wealth to her impressionable charge. From Noreen, Rose learns to take literally the parable of the needles' eyes, "about it's being easier for camels to get through needles' eyes than for rich people to get into the kingdom of heaven" (p. 85) — a belief that leads her to give away her inheritance to build a school in an obscure African country, which ironically burns down a month later, killing all the children. While Rose is clearly ineffectual as an equalizer of wealth, the personal ramifications of her deed are more ambiguous.

In her deliberate choice of an unassuming lifestyle she has built "brick by brick the holy city of her childhood, the holy city in the shape of that patched subsiding house" (p. 63). She has constructed a livable space separate from the sterile environment in which she was reared. Rose's rejection of her unnurturing childhood home, of ostentatious social privilege, of what Simon perceives as "the landscapes of the idle soul" appear "to him as the human, as the lovely, as the loving, as the stuff of life itself" (p. 27). The natural world from which Simon feels himself to be hopelessly cut off is embodied for him in "the soft, full lake of her nature" (p. 92). Simon regards her as a whole person existing in a cozy and livable — albeit worn and shabby — environment, one accurately reflecting her beliefs and ideals. Indeed, one feels strong tonal approval throughout the novel for Rose's "alliance with objects around her" which "irradiated her, transformed her" (p. 63). She succeeds "stone by stone and step by step," in transforming a house into her own: "I carved it out, I created it by faith, I believed in it, and then very slowly, it began to exist. And now it exists. It's like God. It requires faith" (p. 44). Her self and environment are so integrally connected that one becomes a replica of the other: "How can I move house? It's my whole being that's there" (p. 281).

In "her better moments" she believes and takes pride in her progress on this Bunyanesque journey. But she is also acutely aware that identity is not coherent or holistic, and that one always carries around past selves one can no longer remember and would gladly repudiate:

> one would look back and say, Christ, how could I have done that, believed that, been that, with any conviction? And yet, what about those past selves, what permanence, what validity were they ensured? Foundation stones, was an image that had risen to her mind, because she liked the thought of building. (p. 88)

She knows that she can never erase the privilege distinguishing her, that she is, in effect, playing at a working-class life – for she still owns property and has friends and connections, opportunities and outlets unavailable to her neighbors. And that harmony that love-struck Simon sees in her is partly illusory, for her peace is conjoined with irritability; she is subject to moods of despair and a reckless irrationality close to madness. She even attempts suicide, although she has enough sense to have her stomach pumped shortly afterwards. Her longing for histrionic self-sacrifice resurfaces when she momentarily decides, Isaac-like, to give up the children, go to Africa, and travel "the ways of loneliness and extremity." She feels pulled apart by this vision: "she experienced division. But the two sides did not obliterate each other, they collided, they continued to co-exist" (pp. 286–7). Again, the more sensible side of Rose leaves the "white and wailing woman" and goes to pick up her children. As usual in the lives of Drabble's heroines, children are the stabilizing force.

Rose's difficulty in sustaining her chosen life stems from Christopher's interference. But her decision to marry him in the first place is another example of her impulsive and irrational defiance of both her parents and Noreen, and he brings out in Rose a coarseness and earthiness not otherwise apparent:

> She has wanted him for so many reasons, all directly or perversely Noreen-inspired: because he was sexy and undeniable, and crude about it, and anybody less crude she would have been obliged to deny – but with Christopher one

abandoned judgement, one fell, hopelessly, enchanted, into whatever mud or gutter or dark corner or creaking second-hand bed that one could find. (p. 90)

When Christopher is around, Rose coarsens, becoming more foul-mouthed, irritable and unreasonable. Christopher, in turn, becomes violent, and beats her up on several occasions.

Yet Rose agrees finally to live with Christopher again, and in so doing loses the "holy city" she had attempted, like Christian in *Pilgrim's Progress*, to attain. She experiences "her own living death, her own conscious dying, her own lapsing, surely, slowly, from grace, as heaven . . . was taken slowly from her, as its bright gleams faded" (p. 95). She hopes to "weather" into identity like the grotesque stone lion[70] she observes with Emily and Simon at the dog show in the final scene of the novel. And although Simon does observe beauty in that weathering, the toll has been extensive both for Rose personally and for Simon who has depended upon her, "wanted" her, his relationship with her being "a pale, hopeless brightness" in the "ordered darkness" of his own existence (pp. 189, 192).

That Rose and Simon, then, both subside into tolerable mediocrity, stoically sticking to their mates out of a "sense of obligation," has dissatisfied many readers, though it is a characteristic Drabble resolution, part of her pressing realism. The book appears to advocate too much accommodation and self sacrifice, yet Drabble has shown repeatedly that she values such acceptance of responsibilities and limitations, and she also finds such an interpretation "a terribly simple way of reading what is a profound moral dilemma." Rose embodies her most acute examination of "the conflict between old fashioned concepts of virtue and the claims of the self as against claims of other selves." Drabble "deliberately put" her character in a "very theological . . . a jesuitically difficult position as though I stacked the cards so that if one were asking a priest what's the right thing there would be no right answer. And so, I was a bit hard on her."[71] Moreover, she has argued that because the novel "shows people in a state of continual effort," it is not defeatist and depressing. She explains the most problematical issue of the book – Rose's return to Christopher – as a decision which is

> probably mistaken. We see her slightly lacking the strength to cope with the situation she has accepted, and it is on the cards that the marriage will again degenerate into violence, and that they will, again, part. But this does not mean that her motives (or Christopher's, come to that) are in any way base, or that her spirit is defeatist. If she had made a mistake, she will in time recognise it.[72]

> Going back to Christopher means she has failed to solve the problem between what is good for her and what is good for other people.[73]

I think that on some level Drabble herself suspects that the conclusion was wrong for the book: she has candidly admitted that Rose's return to Christopher paralleled her own inability to break with her husband at the time she was writing the novel.[74] While the conclusion can be faulted for seeming to impose a rigid fate on Rose, Drabble's comments demonstrate her belief that her characters can always change, always surprise. Indeed, the secondary characters in *The Needle's Eye* demonstrate this fact. After Simon meets Christopher, for example, he has to abandon the simple view he held of Rose and Christopher and their marriage. Simon would rather not have to cope with Christopher's explanations of himself; he would prefer the image of him created through legal briefs and Rose's fears. But just as Christopher's physical environment – his comfortable, seedy, intimate flat – reminds Simon of Rose's, so too does what he glimpses of Christopher's mental world. Simon learns that Christopher is motivated by "a morality, a set of judgments, a structure as unrealistic and unworldly as Rose's own" (*NE*, p. 55). This view does not negate for Simon (or for the reader) Christopher's behavior as the wife-beater, the child-snatcher; it merely compounds our view of the man, preventing any simple assessment.

Another person with puzzling, contradictory characteristics

is Emily, Rose's best friend. While she shares Rose's "common" beauty, and lives a pleasant, normal, relatively happy life, she also maintains a clandestine relationship with Meyer, an obnoxious, insecure and vicious man, and she "fancies" Christopher, knowing "all too well that it was a combination of boredom and masochism that attracted her." She craves his violence: "she could herself have asked for no greater happiness than to be hit on the head by one of his vicious blows. . . . She would have died happily from his violence, she would have lain down and asked for it" (p. 259). She later rejects such an attraction, looking back on it with "nostalgic amazement that she ever had felt so much in so poor a cause, against her better judgements," for such perverse inclinations and fantasies are strangely aberrant from her "normal" self.

The Needle's Eye, then, dramatizes the confusing mass of shifting characteristics that constitutes personality, and the consequent difficulty of leading a moral and self-directed life. People are shaped by willful self-creation, by unconscious drives, by conditions society, family, other people, and circumstances dictate. They are not wholes, in Drabble's view, but rather are largely images that both they and other people decide they should be. The relationship between these images and some inner core of being is always virtual, always shifting, always problematic; for Drabble does not subscribe to the view that a character can be fixed forever in an epiphanic apotheosis. For this reason, she argues against seeing Rose's decision to return to her husband as irrevocable, or indeed against reading any of her books as definitive statements of her views. She sees her novels, in fact, as created through dialectical oppositions. While in *The Needle's Eye* she arranges things so that the central characters cannot marry, in her next novel, *The Realms of Gold*, "through a lot of tricks"[75] she arranges things so they can.

*

In Drabble's next novel, *The Realms of Gold* (1975), the life of Frances Wingate – who manages to have it all, a professional career, children, love, a healthy resilience, a *joie de vivre* with only periodic occurrences of depression – is played off against the life of her cousin Janet Bird, imprisoned within her tacky house by her insufferable husband, her small baby and her lack of independent self-assertion; against the life of her nephew Stephen, so lacking her zestful enthusiasm for life that he kills both his small baby and himself; against the life of her Great-aunt Constance who suffered the loss of both her illegitimate baby and her estranged, adulterous lover and who finally died of starvation; against the life of her cousin David Ollerenshaw whose solitary self-sufficiency is antithetical to Frances's gregarious existence; and against a host of other characters – Frances's lover Karel Schmidt, his wife Joy, her mother and father, her brother Hugh and his wife Natasha – even relatively minor characters.

This novel is centered on an interplay of ideas which are discussed and acted out by the characters, embodied in images and landscapes, and articulated by the narrator. The novel contrasts two contradictory views of human identity – an essentially nineteenth-century view of individual self-sufficiency and creativity versus a post-modern view of the overriding cultural, historical, familial, social and linguistic forces which shape the individual. In this way the novel functions as a dialogue between traditional and post-modernist narrative techniques.

The novel both constructs and "deconstructs" its realistic base; both uses and calls into question its traditional novelistic conventions. Readers are asked to accept the characters both as real, and as puppets of the narrator. Furthermore, they are invited to view the novelist's and the central character's acts of imagining as parallel acts of creation. The characters discuss explicitly theories of human existence which are dramatized implicitly in their lives. Descriptive space in the novel – especially houses and landscapes – may evoke simultaneously cultural texts, ideological positions, historical places, sociological movements, and psychological states. Much more complex than it at first appears to be, *The Realms of Gold* is one of

Drabble's most interesting blends of the traditional and the modern.

An obtrusive genial narrator, reminiscent of Fielding's or Thackeray's, intermittently shatters the illusion of realism. Assuming a rapport with readers, this storyteller repeatedly calls attention to the craft of the novel and to the imagined lives of the characters, sometimes by admonishing the reader: "Remember him, for it will be some months before he and Frances Wingate meet again" (*RG*, p. 56), sometimes by anticipating probable objections: "And to those who object to too much coincidence in fiction, perhaps one could point out that there is very little real coincidence in the postcard motif, though there are many other coincidences in this book" (p. 224). These erratic disruptions are coupled with dazzling displays of omniscience. The simultaneous action of a number of characters is elaborately charted; the delivery of international mail is perfectly predicted; the fate of Stephen is gloomily anticipated; the thoughts of a host of characters are summarily reported; and limitations are also playfully conceded: "As for Sir Frank Ollerenshaw and Harold Barnard, who knows what they were thinking. Omniscience has its limits" (p. 341). That acknowledgment is revealing. Thackeray may speak of his puppets, and Dickens may address the reader, but a post-modern writer cannot do the same with the same results, for the convention implies certainties no longer certain.[76] Modern skeptical readers may puzzle over this periodic break in the illusion of realism, or they may, like some reviewers, be annoyed and find that such obtrusive coyness damages the novel. I think Drabble creates such a controlling narrative presence in order to undercut its authority and control, to show that indeed "omniscience has its limits" in the modern world, and the modern novel. She has, in effect, turned a nineteenth-century convention into a post-modernist device, establishing the text, at least in part, as a metafiction, a fiction about the writing of fiction.

For example, the narrator at times confesses to being not truly in control of the fate of the characters.[77] She admits, for example, to being torn between "truth, likelihood, and a natural benevolence" when working out their lives, and implies that their fates are "as yet unresolved" as the book proceeds (p. 183). Furthermore, the control she exerts, she is ready to admit, is arbitrary, fanciful, and perhaps tactically ineffective:

> And that is enough, for the moment of Janet Bird. More then enough, you might reasonably think, for her life is slow, even slower than its description, and her dinner party seemed to go on too long to her, as it did to you. Frances Wingate's life moves much faster. (Though it began rather slowly, in these pages – a tactical error perhaps, and the idea of starting her off in a more manic moment has frequently suggested itself, but the reasons against such an opening are stronger, finally, than the reasons for it.) (p. 83)

The narrator claims that David Ollerenshaw, for example, poses particular problems for her craft, and she expounds upon the difficulties of understanding his "character" and integrating his "story" into the narrative: "The truth is that David was intended to play a much larger role in this narrative, but the more I looked at him, the more incomprehensible he became, and I simply have not the nerve to present what I saw in him in the detail I had intended" (pp. 183–4).

The several implicit parallels between the narrator and the central character Frances Wingate further blur the levels of reference and add to the self-reflexiveness of the novel. Frances Wingate's success as an archaeologist is predicated upon her potent imagination: "I imagine a city, and it exists. If I hadn't imagined it, it wouldn't have existed" (p. 34). Similarly the narrator reminds us that the fictional world and its inhabitants she creates are "imagined" into existence. As Frances wonders what to imagine next, so awed is she by her own creative powers, the narrator likewise pauses and looks pleasingly over her creation: "So there you are. Invent a more suitable ending if you can" (p. 56). Both narrator and character can be likened in some ways to the Great Victorians. Like a relic of an earlier age,

Frances is a person of tremendous energy, will and optimism, an archaeologist who ventures out of England to create and to discover new worlds. And, like a narrator of another age, Drabble's narrator boldly spreads her panorama of characters and manipulates their fates. The implication with both is that their self-assertive robustness is not quite a part of modern life or novelistic craft, but resides in earlier nineteenth-century ways and traditions, which they anachronistically yet determinedly carry on.

At the same time the novel and the central character raise some peculiarly modern questions about the interrelationship of perceptions and reality, fact and fantasy; questions that are always lurking within Drabble's fiction. Fiction is a fanciful world in which writers explore real issues which perplex and interest them. And likewise, for Frances Wingate the world of the Phoenicians is a surrogate realm within which she wrestles with some of the same issues which disturb her about her about her own family: its seemingly total lack of distinction. That Frances chooses to study a desert, merchant people rather than more fashionable, accessible, and likeable people such as the Greeks or Romans is not incidental; it grows out of her own psychic needs, for her own North of England people were also unfashionable dwellers in another inhospitable landscape. Frances speculates that she pursues archaeology and her lover Karel history in

> a fruitless attempt to prove the possibility of the future through the past. We seek a Utopia in the past, a possible if not an ideal society. We seek golden worlds from which we are banished, they recede infinitely, for there never was a golden world, there was never anything but toil and subsistence, cruelty and dullness. (p. 124)

Frances sees these utopian "realms of gold,"[78] in other words, as a fantasy, a created past, which she and others attempt to impose upon reality to make it more tolerable, to cover up the truth of "toil and subsistence, cruelty and dullness." The "real" in effect is deformed by the subjective wishes and needs of the perceiver. The Tizouk people Frances reconstructs, justifies, and loves are a composite of the real and the fanciful, fact and fiction, a coming together of real artifacts with an archaeologist's preconceived views which are an outgrowth of her own psychic needs. Such is, in fact, the way that we always perceive the past, filtered through our present needs and perspectives; and such, no doubt, is the filtering process through which the real becomes transformed into the fictional constructs of a writer's world. In this way too, then, the novel functions as a self-reflexive text, archaeology being a surrogate for novel writing, and Frances Wingate for Margaret Drabble.

Also contributing to the novel's multiple levels of reference is its intensive examination of "the effect of landscape on the soul." Indeed the novel traces Frances's second archaeological discovery, the neglected history of her own Ollerenshaw family, the forgotten roots which have so indelibly shaped her being and her fate. Frances believes strongly in the deterministic effect of landscape upon character. She believes that "one can inherit a landscape" and that there is "something positively *poisoning* the whole of South Yorkshire and the Midlands" (p. 100) which flattens its residents out, which has caused in her family a recurrent depression, a history of suicides and madness, a family malady which she has combatted by throwing herself into her work. Frances knows that family, geography, culture, history all contributed to the expansively global space within which she lives: "Generations of her ancestors had gathered stones in those fields. Her grandfather had grown tomatoes and potatoes. Her father had studied newts and become a professor of zoology. And for herself, as a result of their labors, the world lay open" (p. 124). She thinks of herself as the lucky recipient of the painfully slow and sporadic social and cultural evolution of her family.

The Darwinian reverberations of the text are strong,[79] developing some of the determinist reflections of previous novels. The ditch which fascinates Frances as a child becomes the central image. Out of the mud and slime of the ditch her family has crawled in its slow ascent to a higher life. Yet the ditch's water is poisoning, transmitting the inherited family malaise. Frances is subject to periodic bouts of free-floating anxiety and black depression – metaphorically depicted as falling back into "some squalid muddy intersecting gutter or canal, from which she would struggle wisely back to dry land" (p. 14). On the whole she is a Darwinian survivor – a person of "amazing powers of survival and adaptation" – unlike other members of her family. Her life is set in explicit contrast to a number of other less fortunate family members.

A predecessor flattened out – indeed engulfed – by the landscape is Great-aunt Constance, whose death by starvation causes a stir in the press, and embarrassment and sadness in the family. Yet, while Constance's life and death were tragic, she was severed more from the human community than from the natural one, which gently enfolds Mays Cottage where she lived. Frances's visit to Mays Cottage is an important part of her reintegration, her re-rooting of self. It both contrasts with and complements her earlier trip back to her grandparents' home, Eel Cottage, where she and her sister and brother had spent many a summer. For most of her early adult life, Frances has sought to sever herself from this landscape. Yet when she returns to Eel Cottage, early in the novel, she recognizes that the trees and the shape of the roof and windows call up "some corresponding pattern in her mind, its lines were the lines of memory, a shorthand carving, like the graph of her heart or brain, like the points of its movements. There, that shape, imperfectly remembered, and yet perfectly there: an electrocardiogram of her childhood, a map of her past" (p. 116). The precarious situation of Eel Cottage – somewhat anachronistically preserved by a "rum couple" while the evolutionary ditch is hopelessly polluted, and the towns are perceptibly encroaching on it – is reminiscent of Forster's *Howards End*, in which one can see the red smoke of London from the threatened traditional country house. At the end of *The Realms of Gold*, Frances buys from her father Great-aunt Constance's cottage and, if only as a weekend retreat, it becomes a tenuous link with her roots and her family.

The personal and professional alliance of David Olleren-shaw, Frances's cousin, with minerals, rocks and the larger processes of nature contrasts starkly with Frances's alliance with human evolution. While Frances studies human communities, David Ollerenshaw is a successful geologist with a taste for the "dramatic, dynamic and dangerous manifestations of nature"; he seeks out uninhabited, arid, cataclysmic landscapes. Volcanoes satisfy a craving in his soul for the inhuman grandeur of nature: "Man's life span was too short to be interesting: he wanted to see all the slow great events, right to the final cinder, the black hole" (pp. 185, 186). He is sanguine about man's insignificant place in the larger schemes of nature; Frances's nephew Stephen is not. He signals his self-destructiveness through his interest in Freud's concept of the death instinct, and his fascination with a painting by Salvator Rosa of Empedocles jumping into Etna. These works, which are explicitly discussed in the text, are also implicitly embodied in its language and imagery. Like Empedocles, Stephen leaps "unsubdued, into the flames" (p. 349), taking his child: "Stephen and his child disappeared together into the red crater, made one with nature, transformed to black ash" (p. 352). Though grief-stricken over these deaths, Frances feels that they are also a kind of expiatory salvation for herself and her children, who "mercifully, showed no inheritance of the more unwelcome Ollerenshaw traits. Stephen had taken it all away with him" (p. 353).

Janet Bird, the cousin Frances discovers in Tockley in Lincolnshire, is not entirely free of these "unwelcome traits." Desperately bored by her life as a young mother and the wife of an insufferable husband, she is "flattened out" by the landscape, so much so that at times she would "admit to herself that she would have welcomed a cataclysm, a volcano, a fire, an outbreak of war, anything to break the unremitting nothingness of her existence" (p. 134). Instead she stares vacantly into her domestic "volcano" – the small crater in her melted wax candle. Picking up on another metaphorical strain, the narrator links her to her impoverished ancestors: "Stony ground, stony ground, tolled the bells for Janet Bird" (p. 134). Trying to make her semi-detached estate house cozy and individualized, Janet is fastidious to an extreme; "her own polished hygienic box" (p. 288) is a sterile retreat from experience. Yet at the end of the novel, in large part through Frances's example, "Janet came to believe that instead of confronting a life of boredom, she was merely biding her time. . . . Even if the gas mains didn't blow up under Aragon Place, something else might happen, after all" (p. 357).

Janet's fate is left open-ended; Frances Wingate's is not. The strong and privileged member of her family, she continues to be unfairly blessed, looked after by a beneficent destiny, and a benign narrator who pulls the strings to make all well. In the manner of the nineteenth-century novel playfully adopted here, the narrator even looks ahead into the future, foreseeing the marriage of Frances's daughter to Karel's son, and his wife Joy's convenient transformation into a lesbian, as all the obstacles to Frances's happiness drop away. But perhaps Joy's claims upon Karel are too easily diminished and dismissed. Responding to the dissolution of Karel's marriage as one of Drabble's "tricks" to effect the happy ending, readers may again read against the grain, as it were, and balk at the implicit evaluations of the text. Karel Schmidt is a curious contradictory character, capable – in spite of his extreme gentleness, his patient altruism – of periodically beating his wife. While Frances would like to believe that Joy deserves and provokes such behavior, Karel's actions are not easily condoned. He who escaped the concentration camp massacre of his family is both victim and victimizer: unduly put upon by boring and demanding people, insufficiently assertive, yet sporadically violent, impulsive, and imprudent.

Reflecting major movements in English social and cultural history and portraying the individual within a vast complex of interrelating circumstances, *The Realms of Gold* is a profound examination of Frances's queries: "Where does the individual stop and the family begin?" How much can one sever oneself from one's "roots" and create oneself anew? In its wide-ranging examination of the nature of human existence, the novel brings to bear a number of disciplines – archaeology, biology, history, geology, even gynecology. No other novel by Drabble contextualizes the characters in such complex networks of ideology, history, family, culture, and language. No other has such extensive imagistic patterns which skillfully interweave the real and the metaphorical, outer and inner realities. No other is written in such a grandly omniscient way. No other "invents" a more resolved ending or projects more boldly into the future. An impressive novel with a scope unequalled in Drabble's canon, it is overtly controlled and manipulated in a way uncharacteristic of much of Drabble's work. But what is gained in novelistic breadth is in some ways lost in psychological depth, complexity, and resonance, resulting in characterization – particularly that of Frances Wingate – less interesting than earlier, less ambitious novels.

4

URBAN GROUND

Margaret Drabble's two most recent novels differ markedly from her earlier fiction. Although several features initiated in *The Realms of Gold* are continued in *The Ice Age* (1977) and *The Middle Ground* (1980) – the large cast of characters, the simultaneity of action, the omniscient narration – the two later novels are distinguished by a sharp change in focus, from the particular to the general. Drabble here is increasingly preoccupied with the texture of contemporary urban life, including the trends, fads, trappings of mass culture; and the most vividly memorable passages of both books depict the dehumanized, noisy, dirty, ugly and graffiti'd world that is modern urban Britain. The environment in which characters live is largely shaped from without. Houses are islands of selfhood, often insulated retreats from larger forces, and occasionally living circles of human connection and community.

Like their author, the characters, for the most part successful in their professional lives, are now experiencing a midlife reappraisal of self. The old values, ways, and ideas no longer hold, but the new way is not yet clear. They are obsessed less with their pasts than with the quality and significance of the lives they are now leading – lives which strikingly resemble those of their associates. The personal issues which formerly concerned Drabble's characters – relationships to parents, children, husbands and lovers – now generate less tension than do the questions about careers, about the meaning of life and

91

about viable connections to something larger than the self. *The Ice Age* depicts individual characters and the nation in the grip of crises of various kinds – imprisoned, frozen into frustrating inaction; in *The Middle Ground* little seems to be happening, and the characters suffer motionless sameness. In both cases, her people feel out of control, unable to impose a meaningful shape on experience, for the old patterns no longer fit. They feel alternately imprisoned without choice and overwhelmed with the burden of decision-making. The ground is imperceptibly moving from under their feet; they feel themselves suspended, fragmented, disoriented, unsure. Where they had earlier stood upon what seemed to be strongly held values and opinions, nothing now seems certain.

And what is happening to individuals clearly reflects, in turn, what is happening to the British nation as a whole – which is depicted as getting older, tired, staid, facing crises and going through some strange and disorienting metamorphosis. Like other contemporary novelists, Drabble in these books is attempting to engage with the troubled, widely shared social contexts and experiences of urban middle-class life. Perhaps fatigued, as Bernard Bergonzi has suggested in *The Situation of the Novel* (pp. 224–5), by a "fundamental lack of material" and by "run-of-the mill realistic novels" with predictable subjects and plots, some contemporary British novelists have ranged panoramically over British life and "have tried to pin down not just the public events but the shifting sensibility and flavour of the seventies, in very particular phases: 1972 in [Malcolm Bradbury's] *The History Man*, 1975–6 in *The Ice Age*." Depicting the collapse of humanistic values in a determining world, these two novels are similar in their wry and detached portrayal of exemplary men of the age. (Indeed, Drabble told Leon Higdon that she was reading Bradbury's novel when she started hers and "found it almost impossible to put this novel out of my head.") In *The History Man* it is Howard Kirk, the sociologist, who is a product of the liberating 1960s when "everything seemed wide open; individual expectation coincided with historical drive" and who is now swept along by every changing fad and trend, every "plot of historical inevitability." In *The Ice Age* it is Anthony Keating, television journalist turned property speculator in the self-gratifying 1970s, who is similarly a "weed upon the tide of history." To be sure, Howard Kirk is much more unsympathetic than Anthony Keating, in large part because Bradbury, more directly than Drabble, is deliberately challenging some of the conventions and epistemological assumptions of realistic fiction. Both novels, however, are remarkably successful in capturing the texture and tone of life in the 1970s. Other denser, very different works which include a historical sweep and also attempt to sum up the "state of the nation" and the "Englishness" of the English include Angus Wilson's *No Laughing Matter* (1967) and John Fowles's *Daniel Martin* (1977).

Drabble's work is implicitly, perhaps unconsciously self-reflexive. She appears to be struggling for a voice, a method, a form to facilitate the shift from the particular to the general. *The Ice Age* is highly controlled, a visibly plotted work – and so too are the lives of the characters it chronicles; *The Middle Ground* is plotless and shapeless – the novel is losing tension just as the lives of the characters are. But then *The Middle Ground* is a "female" book, a deliberate tribute to Virginia Woolf and the female traditions which link Woolf and Drabble, in a way that *The Ice Age*, with its male protagonist and curious John le Carré ending, is not. As Ellen Cronan Rose has argued, *The Middle Ground* repudiates "the closed narrative mode of 'history' – where patterns are discerned and meaning is fixed" in being a feminine "document"[80] with a feminine ending that is unpredictable, open and full of joyful anticipation: "Anything is possible, and it is all undecided. Everything or nothing. It is all in the future. Excitement fills her, excitement, joy, anticipation, apprehension. Something will happen" (*MG*, p. 270).

This openness to contingency – this refusal to close with a proper Kermodean "sense of an ending" – has distinguished Drabble's best work throughout her career. Behind it lies her repudiation of the modernist/symbolist sense of the Artist as a visionary sage who imposes an imperishable form on "what is past, or passing, or to come." Also behind it lies her modesty as a writer who readily and perhaps sometimes too smugly acknowledges her limitations. Confessions about the inadequacy of her craft to encompass inchoate experience punctuate her novels: "I don't seem to be able to describe how that party was at all" (*SBC*, p. 116); "Lies, lies, it's all lies. A pack of lies" (*W*, p. 84); "The truth is that David was intended to play a much larger role in this narrative, but the more I looked at him, the more incomprehensible he became" (*RG*, pp. 183–4). In *The Middle Ground* Margaret Drabble seems to go a step further by refusing to order her "document" into an exemplary form: "How had she managed to acquire the deadly notion that everything she did or thought had to be *exemplary*, had to *mean something*, not only for herself, but also for that vast quaking seething tenuous mass of otherness, for other people?" Kate Armstrong (the central character) and Margaret Drabble ask: "Shapeless diversity, what was wrong with that?" (*MG*, pp. 224–5).

*

The Ice Age (1977) is about the "freeze" of the mid-1970 recession: Britain is suffering an age of "ice" – variously imaged in the novel by cold, paralysis, imprisonment, forced inaction, death. The individuals are dwarfed by the age which shapes them, the narrative voice which distances them, the inscrutable play of chance and determinism which move them about. Deftly building up a panoramic sense of simultaneity and similarity in part 1, the narrator cuts from one character to another, each, on a single day, attempting to cope with a debilitating crisis – Anthony Keating with a heart attack; Alison Murray with the imprisonment of her daughter Jane in a Balkan country; Kitty Friedmann with the loss of her foot and her husband in an IRA terrorist attack; Len Wincobank with his imprisonment for illegal property speculation; Maureen Kirby, his girlfriend, with his absence and her reduced circumstances. Not only are these individuals stymied by unexpected misfortune, the rest of the nation is summarily included in the "terrible times" which individually and collectively "lay like a fog" over the country, encapsulating England within the icy grip of economic collapse and concomitant paralysis: "A huge icy fist, with large cold fingers, was squeezing and chilling the people of Britain, that great and puissant nation, slowing down their blood, locking them into immobility, fixing them in a solid stasis, like fish in a frozen river" (*IA*, pp. 62–3). Detached, wise, and sometimes wryly bemused by the complaints, perverse adjustments, and rare philanthropy of these distressed Britons, the narrator surveys the "state of the nation":

> Those who had been complaining for the last twenty years about the negligible rise in the cost of living did not of course have the grace to wish that they had saved their breath to cool their porridge, because once a complainer, always a complainer, so those who had complained most when there was nothing to complain about were having a really wonderful time now. . . .
>
> There were, of course, a few perverse souls who enjoyed the prospect of a little austerity. They had been happiest during the war, and had returned to a life of cheese-rind-paring and carrot-growing with alacrity. . . .
>
> There were also the real poor: the old, the unemployed, the undesirable immigrants. . . . Let us not think of them. Their reward will be in heaven.
>
> Finally, there was the small communion of saints, who truly hoped that from this crisis would come a better sharing among the nations of the earth. . . . They tried now to repress their horror and their satisfaction at the unedifying spectacle of the death-throes of greed in their own so-privileged nation. (pp. 62–5)

The "state of the nation" is individualized and particularized in the fate of Anthony Keating, our representative professional middle-class Briton. Growing up "under the massive yellow

95

sandy shadow of the cathedral wall" (p. 20), son of a clergy-man, "reared in an anachronism as an anachronism" (p. 21), Anthony has stumbled into a successful career in broadcast journalism but finds himself in midlife in the mid-1960s "underemployed, bored, and not at all happy in his relation to his work, his country, or the society he lived in: ripe for conversion, to some creed. A political creed, but there wasn't one: a religious creed, but he had had God, along with his father and life in the cathedral close. So what would happen to the vacant space, in Anthony Keating? What would occupy it?" (p. 26). The "vacant space" is occupied by Len Wincobank, who draws him into property speculation. Anthony feels he had before this lived with his "head in a bag — a bag which was taken off only when he got into some nice, safe, familiar, middle-class, intellectual interior." Becoming "at one with the spirit of the age" of the early 1970s, openly participating in the "modern capitalistic economy," Anthony discovers "The Other England" (pp. 31, 34).

But Anthony's career in property is aborted by simultaneous personal and public collapse – a heart attack and the mid-1970s recession. Anthony retreats for recuperation to his newly bought, seventeenth-century house in Yorkshire, High Rook House. Indeed, houses continue as in earlier novels to be refuges and barriers against unpleasant external realities. Ironically, and as Alison Murray says, inconsistently, Anthony Keating in his seventeenth-century house is tempo-rarily shielded from the urban blight – the dislocation and destruction of neighborhoods – that he helps spread through his property speculation.

Alison is deeply upset by the assaulting nature of the urban environment she must pass through on her way back from Walachia, appalled by the dirt of Victoria and St Pancras stations, saddened and bemused by the contrast between the impressive Gothic architecture of the Victorian stations and the grit, rubbish, and seedy, shifting population of these public places: "It can't be like this, thought Alison: how can it have got to be like this? Who has so undermined, so terrified, so threatened and subdued us?" (p. 165). Profoundly unsettling is her attempt to cross an intersection at the city center of Northam, an experience made all the more horrible because a dog which has similarly attempted to cross has been hit by a car. Alison, climbing over the railings, is herself "forced like the dog to pursue her own ends in a hostile environment" (p. 170).

In Drabble's world, as we have seen, there should be an integral connection between people and their houses and environments. Something is terribly wrong, "immoral," Alison senses, when property is viewed as a saleable commodity, and not as a nurturing space of human habitation. Similarly, Maureen is uneasy about the impending relocation of her Aunt Evie to a Council house, feeling that, however shabby and run-down her aunt's present neighborhood is, the living connections she has made with her environment will be irrevocably severed when it is torn down. In this novel no connection links humanistic values and ordinary life. Giles Leggett and, abortively, Anthony Keating are in property speculation for the gambler's thrill, the lure of big profits, and they leave behind them the liberal values they once professed. Some friends such as Linton Hancock, a classics scholar, cling to the old ways: "Unable to adapt, unable to learn new skills, obstinately committed to justifying the old ones" (p. 74). But the humanistic values of the classics are not, through the likes of Linton, infused into modern life; the split is complete. There is no character in this book like Rose Vassiliou of *The Needle's Eye*, who, however ineffectually, attempts to equalize wealth and live in a personal space with communal roots. Nor is there a character here like Frances Wingate of *The Realms of Gold* who can single-handedly oppose the spirit of the times. It is true that Len Wincobank is a potent, aggressive and imaginative man who is genuinely committed to a "material paradise" (p. 126). Child of the working class, he redevelops urban neighborhoods on a grand scale. But he neglects the human scale, let alone the legal one. His opportunistic wheeling-and-dealing land him in Scraby prison, stymied like the other characters and the nation by the unexpected reversal of the booming self-gratifying 1960s and 1970s.

That the English cityscape is shaped in large part by men like Len Wincobank is a reflection on the abnegation of leadership by the professional middle class, the "desperate comfortable lazy liberal folk" that Anthony Keating "had gone into property to avoid: all the smart alecks, all the bitter trendies, all the snipers and laughers and jokers, all the people who spent their time laughing at what they had no hope of understanding" (p. 209), the people who entertainer Mike Morgan berates "for being what they were: drunk, idle, affluent, capitalist, elitist" (p. 210), the people with an impoverished sense of idealism and purpose, the people who seek more and more extreme stimuli to relieve the boredom of their lives. The condition of these middle-aged characters reflects that of England itself: "England, sliding, sinking, shabby, dirty, lazy, inefficient, dangerous, in its death throes, worn out, clapped out, occasionally lashing out" (p. 93). Furthermore, the next generation offers little promise – if Jane Murray is any example, Jane who petulantly claims "it wasn't my fault" that she caused an accident in which two people were killed, Jane who later attempts to starve herself to death out of perverse curiosity: "I did it to see what it would feel like" (p. 276). While Alison hates to entrust the future of the country to people like her daughter, she feels that "she herself was too old: weak, ineffective, impotent. So was Anthony. They had planned to retire, early, from the scene, because they no longer had the energy to deal with daily life" (p. 93).

Yet retirement from the scenes of activity cannot be truly an answer. The omniscient narrator in part 3 stands above the scene, sketching in the fate of the other characters and running through some possible courses of action:

> But what of Anthony Keating and Alison Murray? What will they do? Return to London and the vicissitudes of the market? Farm trout or watercress? Donate High Rook House to the Youth Hostel Association, or transform it into

a home for the handicapped? Will Alison resume her long abandoned career, will Anthony drink himself to death? (pp. 237–8)

But although "they thought of all these things," they "did not have time to choose between them." Just as it seems that perhaps the paralyzing economic recession will be relieved by North Sea oil, so Anthony's perplexing inaction is solved through another unexpected *deus ex machina*: called upon to rescue Jane Murray in Walachia, he inadvertently becomes a British spy and ends up imprisoned, after having successfully ushered Jane out on the last plane to leave.

Exciting as this dramatic and unexpected action is, the perplexing, disquieting spy-thriller ending raises more questions than it answers. Certainly it does not fully answer the question of how people like Anthony and Alison, the educated professional class, could and should live in England. Anthony all too willingly becomes a "weed upon the tide of history," ready to give up his freedom and go where fate may lead him. The central issues the novel raises, but ultimately does not resolve, indeed have to do with the relationship of free will and determinism, chance and destiny. After noting the number of disasters within his immediate acquaintance, one character, Callendar, madly proclaims to his jailmate, Len Wincobank, "Something has gone wrong . . . with the laws of chance." While Callendar's theory is, Len finds, a rather ingenious "way of explaining his own dramatic reversal which would exculpate him from all personal blame" (pp. 162–3), this novel does seriously question where the personal ends and the collective begins.

Alison strives to believe in chance, because she is appalled at the idea of a potent willfulness – either divine or human – which could inexorably shape or maim human lives – such as her daughter Molly's or her sister Rosemary's. She is shaken and upset over her sister's breast cancer, fearing that she somehow was the cause, that Rosemary's jealousy of her inflamed it: "I gave Rosemary cancer of the breast, said Alison to herself, aloud, to see how the words sounded. They did not sound very foolish" (p. 97). She strongly suspects that her daughter Jane's childhood bicycle accident was a willful attempt to wrench Alison's attention from Molly her retarded daughter, just as Jane's later car accident in Walachia was another such attempt. Alison is tempted to believe that "there is no such thing as an accident. We are all marked down. We choose what our own ill thoughts choose for us" (p. 152). To cope with the injustice and the potency of her own identity as a beautiful and talented woman, Alison "had tried to undo herself. She had stripped herself, leaving only her body, a clothes horse, for that she could not relinquish" (p. 187). Afraid of outdoing her husband, her sister, her daughters, she chooses the "nonself," devoting herself to Molly. When she must finally sever herself from her other daughter Jane, she feels she has "wandered into some dangerous territory of the spirit . . . held in some cold grip" (pp. 187–8).

At the end of the novel Alison is free and Anthony imprisoned, but their physical conditions belie their mental attitudes. Anthony explores the relationship of fate and free will from the detached and philosophical perspective imposed upon him by his exile and imprisonment. Quite unexpectedly he thinks one day: "I do not know how man can do without God" (p. 258). Later in prison he reads Boethius and sets out to write a work "to justify the ways of God to man" (p. 286).[81] That Boethius shows up in the prison library is more than coincidental. Anthony, like Boethius, attempts to attribute to an immutable and eternal God a sovereign rule over space and time. What seem to be chance and random accident are only part of a larger providential scheme. Man is too embroiled in the particulars of his personal life and culture to see this larger connectedness. His "consolation" is his "faith" that human life does connect up in meaningful ways, ways beyond his, not God's, apprehension. Anthony, like so many Drabble characters before him, accommodates himself to his situation and in true British fashion "muddles through" both imprisonment and theology.

As the novel cuts back and forth between the particular and the general, the implication is that England, like Anthony, is temporarily "imprisoned" by an unexpected turn of events, but that this stasis provides it, and Anthony, with an opportunity for "self-contemplation" — a chance for a reassessment and realignment of values. Earlier Anthony had expressed faith that

> there would be an answer, for the nation if not for himself, and he saw, as he sat there, some apparition, of this great and powerful nation, a country lying there surrounded by the grey seas, the land green and grey, well worn, long inhabited, not in chains, not in thrall, but a land passing through some strange metamorphosis, through the intense creative lethargy of profound self-contemplation, not idle, not defeated, but waiting still, assembling defences against the noxious oily tides of fatigue and contempt that washed insistently against her shores. (p. 215)

Margaret Drabble seems to share that faith without yet being willing or able to supply the "answer," beyond suggesting that it is ultimately a philosophical or perhaps a theological, rather than a narrowly personal or social, one.[82] The space within which her characters live — while vividly particularized — increasingly opens out to the metaphysical "territory of the spirit."

*

While Drabble's next and most recent novel, *The Middle Ground* (1980), is radically different from *The Ice Age* in shape and structure, it is equally broadly focused upon a number of representative characters. The book is a culmination of Drabble's increasingly explicit concern with the shared social, cultural, and physical environment, another public novel of contemporary history. And, as the phrase "the ice age" triggers a cluster of related images for that novel, so the title of this one imagistically focuses the work upon "middle grounds" — some real, some figurative. It refers most obviously to the metaphorical "middle ground" of life – midlife. The four central characters, Kate, Evelyn, Hugo, and Ted, are all in middle age, all successful professional people with children nearly grown. Like their friends and associates, they have had common experiences, have progressed predictably and successfully through the passages of life and their cultures. Now their lives are gradually assuming a different shape; the figurative "ground" upon which they had been standing seems to be a "draughty open space" (*MG*, p. 16), which is imperceptibly shifting and upsetting the old sureties and patterns:

> The middle years, caught between children and parents, free of neither: the past stretches back too densely, it is too thickly populated, the future has not yet thinned out. No wonder a pattern is slow to emerge from such a thick clutter of cross-references, from such trivia, from such serious but hidden connections. (p. 182)

Meanwhile, the actual "ground" – the environment of London – is also changing, and also at some mid-point in some uncertain transition. The cityscape is cluttered, graffiti'd, bizarre and hostile, an environment in which the characters feel "assaulted all day long," visually, emotionally and even physically. Some of the most vivid passages of the book catalogue this visual assault. Evelyn wonders about the effect of these images upon children:

> What could one expect but delinquency, of children reared amidst such prospects? What images could one expect them to create for themselves? No wonder they dressed in battle-dress, adorned with plate armour of badges on their bosoms and clinking chain mail of staples and safety pins and paper clips. Each day they went into battle, along their own streets. (p. 135)

Evelyn is obsessed, as so many of Drabble's characters are, by the inevitable formative effect of environment upon character. Landscapes become internalized, inexorably shaping the soul. But retreat to the country is not possible, and Evelyn does not close herself off from the environment. She believes that a "conspiracy of faith" is necessary to make cities safe: "We ought all to behave *as though* we trust one another, for the more often ordinary people walk across the Heath, the safer it is, the more we use public transport, the safer it will be" (p. 219). And when Evelyn herself is assaulted – while on her round to one of her social service clients, she is hit in the face by a bottle of cleaning fluid – she "does not spread alarm." She continues to be assured that people create a web of caring and concern which makes society tolerable. While she recovers, her injury at least temporarily shakes the faith of her friends and family in their safety and immunity from random violence, from an aggressively hostile and threatening environment. Kate thinks:

> what if each act of personal violence were after all an expression, a culmination of all that vaguely directed ill-will, hatred and frustration, of the terror we each now feel when walking down a concrete underpass, when we fumble for a key on our own doorstep with the sound of footsteps behind us, when an unknown car pulls up at the kerb? Belfast, Beirut, Baghdad. And was this London, a bed-sitter in flames, a girl from Bradford, an insane Jamaican, a child from East Pakistan? No, surely not, surely not. (p. 223)

Kate is bemused by the heterogeneous people involved in the incident. It is one of the many episodes in this book that highlight the increasingly international space in which modern Britons live, and which has begun to globalize a good deal of British fiction from the 1970s onwards. England itself no longer feels domestic. The point is emphasized in the experience and in the technique of the novel. Kate's narrowly western frame of reference is expanded by interaction with her Iraqi house guest, Mujid. Hugo has had disquieting international experiences; while on an anthropological study in Iraq, he was held prisoner in the Kurdish battle for independence, and while a war correspondent he lost an arm in Eritrea. Hugo wonders if global perspectives are not now imperative: "Will anyone ever again be able to write, with confidence, a book that assumes the significance of one culture only, will anyone ever again be able to stand upright in one nationality?" (p. 170).

But not only does the "ground" upon which the characters must stand spread out internationally; it must also reach down to metaphoric depths – into the sewers. One of the strangest features of the book is Kate's attraction to the sewers. As a child she had enjoyed putting her face to the grating and taking a good sniff. She has to restrain herself from repeating this act as an adult: "Oh, God, Kate sighed. She'd never read Proust, but she'd heard of Proust's madeleine. How typical of her, to have chosen a sewage bank for such stirrings, instead of a nice cake and a nice cup of tea" (p. 117). Clearly her attraction to the sewers is linked to her past: her father was a sewage superintendent and she grew up in the shadow of the sewage bank. As the "sewer connection" develops in the novel, the literal again becomes the figurative; the sewers connote the "underground" of Kate's personality and background, the part of herself – "the tangled roots in her heart" (p. 117) – she severed to make her above-the-ground self. Sewers and roots are conflated; both are images of the underground of personality, "the dirty tangled roots of childhood twisted back for ever and ever, beyond all knowing. Impacted, interwove, scrubby, interlocked, fibrous, cankerous, tuberous, ancient, matted" (p. 131). Kate suspects that "perhaps so close an infantile connection with sewage would be bound to have some effect on the psyche?" She flirts with psychoanalytical explanation but gives up in despair, "oh dear, oh dear, thought Kate . . . the trouble is, anything *could* mean anything. Or its opposite" (pp. 131–2). Continuing the anal suggestiveness is Kate's description of her own success as "turning shit into gold." For Kate has learned early to tell truthful, witty stories "translated into art" out of the "good material" of her dreary childhood world.

Readers may here find that the borders between fictional and real "ground" are again somewhat indeterminate; for there are striking parallels between this character and her author. Both

Kate Armstrong and Margaret Drabble have generated their early work out of their identities as women, and were viewed as writers of women's works, as champions of feminist perspectives. Only now, Kate (and, one suspects, Margaret Drabble)[83] is fatigued with "peddling opinions." Kate claims to be "bloody sick of bloody women. . . . I'm sick to death of them, I wish I'd never invented them, but they won't just go away because I'm tired of them. Will they?" (p. 8). Both have found that their breadth of class experience has proved to be eminently valuable: "Her lower-class-middle-class origins, onto which she grafted the language and opinions of the artistic and articulate middle class, proved an invaluable asset; she could communicate with a large audience" (p. 39). Kate's early interest in the personal and the unique has been gradually replaced by a fascination for the general ("she found herself entranced by trends, graphs, percentages, emerging patterns, social shifts" (p. 52)), just as Drabble's novels have increasingly turned to the social scene rather than to the individual psyche. Kate feels that she is now writing about subjects "which were really beyond her scope" (p. 59); and some reviewers and critics have had the same opinions about Margaret Drabble's latest work. Where earlier life had for Kate easily yielded its patterns, easily translated into language, now Kate struggles with the difficulty of shaping life into meaningful patterns, into pithy and witty disquisitions. Finally, fatigued by the effort and dubious of the results, she tells herself, "Enough of patterns, she'd spent enough time looking for patterns and trends. . . . Shapeless diversity, what was wrong with that?" (p. 225). The "shapeless diversity" Kate embraces is an appropriate term with which to characterize the novel's structure.

Unlike her earlier works, Margaret Drabble here creates a plotless novel with minimal drama, intensity, and psychological depth, one which relies upon summary to a striking degree. Tension and drama which resided in earlier books in tortured psyches, adulterous liaisons, or two-women relationships are not here developed, although we still have the duress, the adultery, and the relationships. The difference is that tense, painful, drama-filled experiences are for the most part included in the background summary, and not the present time of the novel, which instead focuses on inconsequential social gatherings or snatches of ordinary work on ordinary days. In fact, in its focus on the ordinary and the trivial and in its culmination in a party, the novel is somewhat reminiscent of some of Virginia Woolf's novels, especially *Mrs Dalloway* and *To the Lighthouse*.

And Kate, thinking of Mrs Dalloway, sets off in explicit imitation of her to buy some flowers for the party.[84] While Mrs Dalloway courts high society, Kate prefers the "companionable gutter" (p. 148). While Mrs Dalloway finds her identity in her marital status, Kate is content to be single. While Mrs Dalloway enjoys the uplifting texture of London life – the striking of Big Ben, the movement of the King through the city, the aeroplane overhead, Kate prefers to look down, "exploring her own weird shabby impossible sprawling unstylish noisy underground world" (p. 185). Yet both Kate and Mrs Dalloway are seen by close male friends, Hugh Mainwaring and Peter Walsh, as alternately vain and shallow, beautiful and true – for in both books the psychological space between individuals is filled with flickering conjecture, inconstantly held opinions, shifts of mood, might-have-beens, as in this very Woolfian scene with Hugh and Kate:

"How lucky we are," said Kate, still staring back, "that we should each think each other so wonderful." And she got up, and started to wipe the table, sweeping the crumbs carefully into her open palm, and Hugo, watching her, thought that sublime was indeed the word, for at such moments something in Kate seemed to shimmer just beneath or above the surface, *sub lumen*, a breaking light, and she had this knack, this gift, for catching a little of it and bringing it, but just, but just within range, like an astral halo flickering on the sight, calling from him a corresponding gleam: a bright person, an angel in the house, among the crumbs and dustbins and fish heads. Ah, folly, thought Hugo, as he watched, she is just a woman, and a rather gullible, foolish, self-centred vain woman at that: and Kate, washing her hands under the rubber swizzle tap, looked back at Hugo, his delicate, intellectual, ascetic features, so elegant, so precise, so finely drawn, and thought, after all, Hugo is only a man, and rather a selfish, dangerous, and self-deluding one at that. (p. 254)

What Woolf calls the "semi-transparent envelope" Drabble describes as "the space between them, solid but transparent, as thin and clear as water. Unlived lives, roads not taken, roads blocked, children not born, ghosts and shadows" (p. 253).

The comparison with Woolf can be extended. Kate, like Mrs Ramsay in *To the Lighthouse*, is "wound about" in the hearts and lives of her family and associates. Like Mrs Ramsay, she is intimately connected with the "living" house (p. 270) in which she resides, generating a circle of connectedness, a small space of harmony, in a world of seeming disconnection. Like Mrs Ramsay, Kate has brief moments of peace, of seeing life steadily and seeing it whole:

> looking around her family circle, feeling as she sat there a sense of immense calm, strength, centrality, as though she were indeed the centre of a circle, in the most old-fashioned of ways, a moving circle – oh, there is no language left to describe such things, we have called it all so much in question, but imagine a circle even so, a circle and a moving sphere, for this is her house and there she sits, she has everything and nothing, I give her everything and nothing. (p. 268)

The house in Drabble's work, as in Woolf's, is an objectivization of the self, an external expression of personality, and both writers are ultimately concerned with the relationship of this personal space to a larger social and metaphysical connectedness. As in *To The Lighthouse*, houses here are islands of the self in a seemingly hostile and indifferent world, one made all the more perplexing, jumbled, and disorienting by the urban environment. Yet Evelyn and Kate observe that if one gets far enough above the cityscape, as from the perspective of Evelyn's hospital room, the London scene seems not at all decaying and hopeless, but varied, vital, and endlessly self-renewing: reflective of a greater human connectedness:

> The old and the new side by side, overlapping, jumbled, always decaying, yet always renewed; London, how could one ever be tired of it? How could one stumble dully through its streets, or waste time sitting in a heap staring at a wall? When there it lay, its old intensity restored, shining with invitation, all its shabby grime lost in perspective, imperceptible from this dizzy height, its connections clear, its pathways revealed. (p. 238)

Physical space again suggests the metaphysical: "The aerial view of human love, where all connections are made known, where all roads connect?" (p. 238). Kate, saying "I can't believe that this is all" (p. 254), retains faith in a "higher space" beyond the "middle ground" of human comprehension, where spiritual connection exists.

This novel undoubtedly has a rich spatial texture through which are raised many of the thematic issues that obsess Drabble: the relationship of the individual to larger shaping institutions, contexts, and forces. Yet *The Middle Ground* is not finally a compelling book to read. Boldly abandoning so many of the conventional narrative and dramatic techniques that usually characterize her fiction, Drabble has not replaced them with engaging alternatives. The mundane and trivial are not, for example, ordered with the poetic resonances of Virginia Woolf's work. In spite of its metaphorical suggestiveness, *The Middle Ground* is flat, lacking intensity. One senses that this novel represents a transitional "middle ground" in Drabble's continuing artistic development.

Drabble herself claims the book was a somewhat "contradictory" attempt to depict the heterogeneity of modern urban life using a too narrow focus, showing how in one section of a city "all sorts of things crowd and all sorts of simultaneous things are going on." She would now like to attempt a more ambitious novel doing the same sort of thing on a bigger scale. Although she doesn't know what her next book will be about ("there's been a lot happening in the past five years that I haven't used"), she is fascinated by the technical problem connected with writing a modern *Middlemarch*:

> There must be some answer to the omniscient narrator and the interconnected articulation of society today which is different and which she [George Eliot] does so well. I'm interested in the way society is either pocketed or interlocking . . . which bits overlap and which bits can never overlap, or only can overlap through crisis or disaster or things going wrong.

Such a book, she speculates would require "a different narrative style altogether," one which could portray a "kind of map of people's consciousness."[85] She is open to whatever form or style might evolve from this preoccupation.

And perhaps the dominant impression I have from my recent conversation with Margaret Drabble is her flexibility and openness to contingency both in her life and her fiction. One feels that she, like Kate Armstrong, faces "what next?" with good-humored bemusement, anticipation and receptivity. The view that she is a fictional and ideological traditionalist clinging to pre-modernist values and ways of perceiving and writing is quite wrong: "In sociological and economic terms things would have been worse for me personally so I'm not going to deplore the passing of a tradition in which I would have been a cook-housekeeper." She doesn't adhere to a liberal humanism disconnected from modern realities. In fact, she finds modern theories which emphasize the collective grounds of human behavior much more "challenging" and valuable than those which overemphasize the pre-eminence of the individual consciousness. We may have "too developed a sense of one person's rights rather than of group rights, which doesn't mean I'm an aggressive Marxist, it simply means that I find more of value in looking at collective thinking than some people who regret the decline of liberal humanism." In *The Ice Age* she was trying to show how a liberal humanist like Anthony Keating "saw through the absolute pointlessness of a lot of what he was doing and decided that, in fact, he wasn't in touch with what was happening at all, although he spent all of his time making television programs about what was happening." He was right, in her opinion, to cut himself off from the "comfortable lazy liberal folk": "you'd learn a lot more by taking a risk or two yourself in what he rather romantically conceived of as the 'real' world." This does not mean that Margaret Drabble welcomes with open arms all aspects of modern life. She, like her characters, deplores rampant commercialism, random violence and other dehumanizing aspects of mass culture, but having what she terms an "insatiable curiosity" about life, she is interested to see what is "brewing," what English society is becoming. If it is losing some of its traditional "Englishness" and becoming something else – so be it. She welcomes the "broadening" of consciousness, the greater sense of international "community." She does not believe in the inevitability of decline, "except perhaps in the long term, that the planet is cooling." Rather, she characterizes herself as an optimist who looks at her children and says, "that's fine, that's absolutely fine." Some things have grown better, in her opinion, such as the relationship between the sexes and educational opportunities. Above all else, however, she is anxious to de-emphasize her role as public seer and to disclaim the view that her fiction is exemplary, closed discourse on what should be. She sees herself not as an advocate but as an "inquiring mind," a "free observer": "I suppose I think the less committed one is personally, the freer one is to make these observations . . . standing on a fixed point" with "vested interest" is "dangerous." She looks on life as a metaphoric search or journey and the function of the novel, in her opinion, is to show possibilities rather than creeds for living: "to explore new territory. To extend one's knowledge of the world. And to illuminate what one sees in it." Each book is "a little more territory gained."

The new territory she is now exploring has radically expanded beyond the solipsistic "bird-cages" of her early fiction. Drabble is now less concerned with dramatizing the lives of unique individuals than she is with trying to capture a sense of the general, the representative. What is most successful about her more recent fiction, I think, is its evocation of the images and flavor of contemporary urban space: the buildings, the streets, the stray dogs, the graffiti, the noises, the heterogeneous mix of people. Joyce Carol Oates is right, I believe, in saying that Drabble captures "the tone of contemporary English culture."[86] Indeed, Phyllis Rose has argued that Drabble is "becoming the chronicler of contemporary Britain, the novelist people will turn to in a hundred years from now to find out what things were, the person who will have done for late twentieth-century London what Dickens did for Victorian London, what Balzac did for Paris."[87] Whether Drabble can incorporate these authentic images of contemporary English culture into a fiction that is vibrant remains to be seen. Broader is not necessarily better. Social scope does not always compensate for the loss of psychological depth, or the loss of unique particularity. I especially regret the smugness and complacency of Drabble's successful women like Frances Wingate and Kate Armstrong: the feminist discourse is no longer double-voiced and searching. Perhaps Drabble has personally worked through feminist issues so satisfactorily that they no longer generated the tensions which have enriched her fiction. Although she does not believe that fiction must necessarily grow out of personal conflict, the most successful kind so often does. She is now voicing communal concerns, communal conflict. It is a voice she hasn't yet quite found, however interesting her attempts have been. I think it a difficult voice to find because her work is in many ways less resonant when it is more explicit, when metaphors are on the surface rather than embedded, when conclusions are drawn, characters "pegged", judgments made. She is also experimenting, a little uneasily, with different kinds of novelistic structure – a tight plot for *The Ice Age*, a loose form for *The Middle Ground*: "And I am now thinking that I must write a structured one next time, to tidy it

111

up,"[88] says congenitally dialectical Margaret Drabble, never one to be locked in the same position for long.

I expect she will find an appropriate style and structure for her later fiction. She is fortunately situated between and nurtured by many different contextual worlds be they determined by gender, education, geography, social class, or economic conditions; her attempt to "only connect " these disparate perspectives, along with her willingness to accept what she finds – even if it is "shapeless diversity" – account for both the generating energies and the equivocal tensions of her fiction. Certainly, the wit, the gentleness, the wisdom, and the insistent moral discrimination which infuse all her fiction will continue to draw countless readers to her works.

NOTES

1 Rosalind Miles, *The Fiction of Sex: Themes and Functions of Sex Difference in the Modern Novel* (Plymouth: Vision, 1974), p. 168.

2 Unpublished interview with David Leon Higdon, September 1979. I thank Professor Higdon for kindly letting me see this material.

3 My commentary is based on and tempered by my unpublished interview with Drabble on 19 June 1984. I also try to give credit to the many interviews I have read which have contributed to my general knowledge of Drabble.

4 Interview with John Clare, "Margaret Drabble's Everyday Hell," *The Times*, 27 March 1972, p. 6.

5 Nancy S. Hardin, "An Interview with Margaret Drabble," *Contemporary Literature*, 14 (Summer 1973), p. 289.

6 Dee Preussner, "Talking with Margaret Drabble," *Modern Fiction Studies*, 25 (1979–80), p. 566.

7 Joanne V. Creighton, "An Interview with Margaret Drabble," in Dorey Schmidt (ed.), *Margaret Drabble: Golden Realms* (Edinburg, Texas: Pan American University Press, 1980), p. 29.

8 Interview with Barbara Milton, "Margaret Drabble: The Art of Fiction LXX," *Paris Review*, 20 (Fall–Winter 1978), p. 54.

9 Drabble made these observations and comments to me on 19 June 1984.

10 Iris Rozencwajg, "Interview with Margaret Drabble," *Women's Studies*, 6 (1979), pp. 339, 335.

11 Hardin, op. cit., p. 278.

12 Margaret Drabble, "The Writer as Recluse: The Theme of Solitude in the Works of the Brontës," *Brontë Society Transactions*, 16, 4 (1974), p. 259.

13 Comments to me on 19 June 1984.

113

14 Creighton, op. cit., p. 24.
15 Interview with Juliet A. Dusinberre, "A. S. Byatt," in Janet Todd (ed.), *Women Writers Talking* (New York and London: Holmes & Meier, 1983), pp. 190–1.
16 Hardin, op. cit., p. 277.
17 Interview with Diana Cooper-Clark, "Margaret Drabble: Cautious Feminist," *Atlantic Monthly*, 246 (November 1980), p. 74.
18 Milton, op. cit., p. 569.
19 Preussner, op. cit., p. 575.
20 Comments to me on 19 June 1984.
21 Cooper-Clark, op. cit., p. 75.
22 Interview with Peter Firchow, "Margaret Drabble," in *The Writer's Place: Interviews on the Literary Situation in Contemporary Britain* (Minneapolis: University of Minnesota Press, 1974), p. 105.
23 Cooper-Clark, op. cit., p. 72.
24 Firchow, op. cit., p. 105.
25 Cooper-Clark, op. cit., pp. 72, 75.
26 In *Arnold Bennett* (London: Weidenfeld & Nicolson, 1974), Drabble says: "To Bennett, as to Lawrence, houses expressed souls. People were not disembodied spirits, and the houses they built were as much a part of them as their bodies" (p. 31).
27 Margaret Drabble, "The Author Comments," *Dutch Quarterly Review of Anglo-American Letters*, 5 (1975), p. 36.
28 Malcolm Bradbury and David Palmer (eds), "Preface," in *The Contemporary English Novel* (London: Arnold, 1979), p. 11.
29 A. S. Byatt, "People in Paper Houses: Attitudes to 'Realism' and 'Experiment' in English Postwar Fiction," in Bradbury and Palmer (eds), op. cit., pp. 21, 24.
30 Elizabeth Fox-Genovese, "The Ambiguities of Female Identity: A Reading of the Novels of Margaret Drabble," *Partisan Review*, 46, 2 (1979), pp. 234–48.
31 Cooper-Clark, op. cit., p. 71.
32 Firchow, op. cit., p. 107.
33 Elaine Showalter, *A Literature of Their Own: British Women Novelists from Brontë to Lessing* (Princeton, NJ: Princeton University Press, 1977), pp. 264, 265, 296–7.
34 The term is used by Susan Snaider Lanser and Evelyn Torton Beck, "(Why) Are There no Great Women Critics?" in Julia A. Sherman and Evelyn Torton Beck (eds), *The Prism of Sex: Essays in the Sociology of Knowledge* (Madison, Wisc.: University of Wisconsin Press, 1977), p. 86.
35 Margaret Drabble, "A Woman Writer," *Books*, 11 (Spring 1973), p. 6.

36 Ellen Cronan Rose, *The Novels of Margaret Drabble: Equivocal Figures* (Totowa, NJ: Barnes & Noble, 1980), p. 129.

37 "I have been living for the past year or so in the company of some strange women whose obscure lives haunt me, depress me, and occasionally, unexpectedly cheer me. They are writers whose minor works and lives I've been reading for the revision of 'The Oxford Companion to English Literature,' on which I'm now engaged. . . . Well, it is obvious why they concern me. I ask myself if there is anything representative, necessary in their odd destinies, any linking thread, or are they merely causalities, each perishing alone?" (Margaret Drabble, "Gone but Not Quite Forgotten," *New York Times Book Review*, 25 July 1982, p. 6).

38 "Quite a lot of writers I have never read at all, and now I feel I *would* have been influenced by them if I *had* read them – people like Virginia Woolf I never read a word of until about two years ago. It's funny I completely missed her. She was very unfashionable here in the fifties and sixties, and I just never read a word, and now I *feel* as though I've been influenced but I can't have been, if you know what I mean. It's strange" (Rozencwajg, op. cit., p. 336).

39 Firchow, op. cit., p. 114.

40 Review of *Arnold Bennett: A Biography*, in *The Times Literary Supplement*, 12 July 1974, p. 737.

41 "The New Victorians: Margaret Drabble as Trollope," in Schmidt (ed.), op. cit., pp. 168–77.

42 Firchow, op. cit., p. 117.

43 Fox-Genovese, op. cit., p. 235. Also Charles Burkhardt, "Arnold Bennett and Margaret Drabble," in Schmidt (ed.), op. cit., p. 96: "One is hard put at times to distinguish between Drabble and the classier soap opera or women's magazine."

44 Drabble, "A Woman Writer," p. 6.

45 "'Tis just like a summer bird cage in a garden: the birds that are without despair to get in, and the birds that are within despair and are in a consumption for fear they shall never get out" (*The White Devil*, I.ii). Moreover, Drabble has said about her frequent bird images: "The spirit of a person is like a bird trapped in his body. The cage is the body – definitely a Platonic notion" (Hardin, op. cit., p. 287). See Ellen Moers, *Literary Women* (Garden City, NY: Doubleday, 1976), pp. 243–51, who argues that the caged bird is pervasive throughout women's literature as "a metaphor that truly deserves the adjective female."

46 Rose, op. cit., p. 107, argues convincingly that Simone is a caricature of Simone de Beauvoir.

47 Drabble has frequently disparaged the craftsmanship of her early

novels, particularly *A Summer Bird-Cage*, which she claims "began kind of like writing a long letter to somebody. I began on page one and it kind of – it's incredibly rambling and desultory, *The Summer Birdcage* [sic]. I look at it and I think, Oh God, I might at least have tried" (Rosencwajg, op. cit., p. 343). When asked if this narrative interruption was a conscious decision she said, "It certainly wasn't. I don't know. I was just rattling along. . . . I imagine that what happened was that I thought, oh heavens, I better explain what's going on all the while and where he is and what she's up to, and it seemed to me a perfectly acceptable way of doing it. I'm sure it wasn't anything more profound than that" (Creighton, unpublished interview, 4 September 1979).

48   Rose, op. cit., pp. 7–15, offers a fascinating discussion of food in the novel proposing that Emma in denying her body is displaying the symptoms of anorexia nervosa.

49   The water imagery is also, of course, symbolic of female sexuality. In *The Waterfall* Jane Gray's first sexual orgasm is a "waterfall," in which she finds herself "down there at last in the water and not high up in my lonely place" (p. 150). Emma's "terrestrial" rootedness, her cautious guarding of the river bank lest her daughter "fall in," is one of her many expressions of inhibited sexuality.

50   More than qualified acceptance of Emma is expressed by Valerie Grosvenor Myer, *Margaret Drabble: Puritanism and Permissiveness* (New York: Barnes & Noble, 1974), p. 19, and Marion Vlastos Libby, "Fate and Feminism in the Novels of Margaret Drabble," *Contemporary Literature*, 16, 2 (1975), p. 178, each of whom feel that Emma grows into acceptance and self-knowledge. Much harsher are the judgments of Dee Preussner, "Patterns in *The Garrick Year*," in Schmidt (ed.), op. cit., pp. 117–37, who finds that "Emma has no essential self, but remains an accumulation of roles," and Ellen Cronan Rose who finds her "still a divided self" (op. cit., p. 14).

51   See, for example, Nancy S. Hardin, "Drabble's *The Millstone*: A Fable for Our Times," *Critique*, 15, 1 (1973), pp. 22–34.

52   See, for example, Susan Spitzer, "Fantasy and Femaleness in Margaret Drabble's *The Millstone*," *Novel*, 11 (Spring 1978), pp. 227–45.

53   Drabble in the introduction to the 1970 edition of *The Millstone* says the title refers to Christ's words: 'Whoso shall offend one of these little ones which believes in me, it were better that a millstone were handed about his neck, and that he were drowned in the depth of the sea" (Matt. 18:6). In attempting to explain her

intention she said: "I don't know what I intended actually, but I think it was kind of a double reference. The child was both a millstone and also a salvation because once it became obvious to Rosamund that she couldn't suffer any more harm from the child, the millstone was lifted from her" (Hardin, interview, op. cit., p. 280).

54   Other allusions include Samuel Daniel's "The Complaint of Rosamund," for Rosamund reads Daniel for her dissertation. Although her salvation through her illegitimate child contrasts with the earlier Rosamund's punishing death for hers, both women find their experience has "meaning."

55   Spitzer, op. cit.

56   Creighton, op. cit., pp. 20–1.

57   Rose, op. cit., pp. 24–5. However, about Rosamund, Drabble said to me: "I certainly know, as the narrator behind the narrator," but "even she knows she is diffident beyond all bounds of normal behavior. . . . She's very much in the trap of being her parents' child and unable psychologically to become herself" (Comments to me, 19 June 1984).

58   While I find his work interesting, it will be obvious that I don't totally subscribe to Holland's model(s) of psychoanalytic literary response: *The Dynamics of Literary Response* (New York: Oxford University Press, 1968); *5 Readers Reading* (New Haven, Conn.: Yale University Press, 1975). I see the oral fantasy in this novel as part of the conscious fictive "reality" of Jane's (and James's) character. Although James's motivation is outside the scope of my discussion, I would like to note that he is attracted to Jane largely because she has just had a baby. He himself plays the infant by chastely clinging to her in her wet and warm childbirth bed. In short, his gratifications too seem to be predominantly oral not genital.

59   Drabble herself finds "despicable" the way Jane "does manipulate and play her cards, but there's something I rather admire about the out and out way she goes about it when she's got it." Drabble says one "can't believe a word of what she's said" since she's admitted to manipulating the evidence. Jane is "very amoral," both "overtly and covertly manipulative. She knows that if she sits and waits somebody will come and rescue, and it is very attractive just sitting there and waiting. So I think she has no aspirations towards being good. . . . She wants to write and she knows that she has to maintain freedom within herself, not expose herself to people who are going to mess her up, so she just waits for what suits her. . . . I think Jane is somebody whose sexual nature is so demanding: it has been denied so long, that

she'll wait for the right thing and then she'll just take it. She's interested in not appearing to be the guilty party, so she drove Malcolm out of the house and then sat and waited. Very self-centered behavior. . . . I think she's changed [by the end] in that she's been out and about a bit. I think she's still very selfish and she knows she is, but she probably thinks her talent justifies a certain selfishness. . . . She accepts that she's not all that nice and that she needn't even pretend to be and that life isn't very nice. In fact, that life is more or less exactly as she'd always thought it was, not very nice but rather more exciting and rewarding than she had thought" (Comments to me on 19 June 1984).

60 Byatt, op. cit., p. 34.
61 Bradbury and Palmer (eds), "Preface," op. cit., p. 13.
62 Higdon, op. cit.,
63 Preussner, op. cit., p. 568.
64 Noted by David Leon Higdon, *Shadows of the Past in Contemporary British Fiction* (London: Macmillan, 1985), p. 209.
65 Drabble calls her "the worst mother in my novels," and says that she was "modeled on my grandmother who made my mother's life a misery" (Milton, op. cit., p. 56).
66 Drabble's extra-textual assessment of Clara is harsh: "I don't *like* her very much, I think she's my most unsympathetic heroine, in many ways — she's an elitist at heart . . . she's very tough" (Rosencwajg, op. cit., p. 338). She has also said: "She's going to turn into something fearsome, I think. I rather dread her future" (Hardin, interview, op. cit., p. 278).
67 Drabble, "The Author Comments," p. 36.
68 Ibid.
69 Monica Lauritzen Mannheimer, "The Search for Identity in Margaret Drabble's *The Needle's Eye*," *Dutch Quarterly Review of Anglo-American Letters*, 5 (1975), p. 34.
70 The lion, symbol for England, is here made "a beast of the people," just as Rose is a rose of the people. In this novel, Drabble skillfully makes common symbols uniquely her own.
71 Comments to me on 19 June 1984.
72 Drabble, "The Author Comments," p. 37.
73 Comments to me on 19 June 1984.
74 Hardin, interview, op. cit., p. 277.
75 Drabble, "The Author Comments," p. 38.
76 Yet when I asked Drabble if she found this narrator an "anachronistic convention," she said: "Not really. A lot of writers do it nowadays. Doris Lessing does it quite a lot. She does so much else that people tend not to notice it. It seems to me a very natural way to write. I tend to look upon everything else as the deviation.

118

Everybody knows the writer is there — why shouldn't he say so? It seems very artificial, in a way very pretentious, to pretend that there is no writer, and the writer is a person, and to obliterate the writer from the frame seems to be rather odd. You could say it is like a cameraman showing bits of the camera or showing the other camera. I'm surprised it's not done more, because it seems to be so much a natural way to tell a story" (Creighton, op. cit., p. 18).

77 Drabble carefully distinguishes herself as author from her narrators: "My narrator, not I, is more of an observer, who is sometimes astonished by what is going on. As indeed one is in real life" (Cooper-Clark, op. cit., p. 75).

78 This phrase, of course, comes from Keats's poem, "On first looking into Chapman's Homer." See Pamela S. Bromberg, "Romantic Revisions in Margaret Drabble's *The Realms of Gold*," in Schmidt (ed.), op. cit., pp. 48–65, for a discussion of Drabble's "revisionary exploration" of romantic notions of the "poetic imagination." Also see Nora F. Stovel, "Margaret Drabble's Golden Visions," *ibid.*, pp. 3–17, for a discussion of the concept of a golden world in a number of Drabble's books as "the embodiment of her ideal world of the imagination, a projection of the artist's inner vision."

79 Interestingly, Drabble claims she had not read *The Origin of Species* before she wrote the novel. But after a critic had pointed out the connection, she read it and discovered that the critic "was absolutely right. I mean, there was the very bank, and of course the book is about evolution. I hadn't thought of connecting the octopus and newts to these strange forms of life. But from the critic's point of view, the comments she was making were valid. She thought I had read *The Origin of Species*. But for me, the connection was to the unconscious" (Cooper-Clark, op. cit., p. 74).

80 "Drabble's *The Middle Ground*: 'Mid-life' Narrative Strategies," *Critique*, 23, 3 (1982), pp. 69–82.

81 His statement, of course, echoes Milton's in *Paradise Lost*. In other ways as well Milton is recalled: one of the epigraphs to the volume is the famous passage from *Areopagitica*: "Me thinks I see in my mind a noble and puissant Nation rousing herself like a strong man after sleep, and shaking her invincible locks." The other epigraph is Wordsworth's exhortation "Milton! Thou shouldst be living at this hour: England hath need of thee." The implication is that England needs to be aroused out of its icy paralysis by such visionary faith: "give us manners, virtue, freedom, power," Wordsworth and Margaret Drabble plead.

82   Although Drabble admits to having "great faith in the British nation. One becomes patriotic under pressure, and I do think that there's a wonderful sense of solidarity and a dislike of pure materialism in this country which I like very much. . . . We just keep on going. We don't have revolutions, and we don't throw people in the barricades; we don't become violent on the street very readily, and I can't see this changing. . . . There is a low expectation in this country which is maddening in many ways; it infuriates Anthony Keating, but nevertheless it is a great safeguard, because you don't start throwing yourself out of the city windows when things go wrong. You just accept and carry on" (Creighton, op. cit., pp. 30–1).

83   Indeed, she admits to being "fed up" with women. Mel Gussow, "Margaret Drabble: A Double Life," *New York Times Book Review*, 9 October 1977, pp. 40–1.

84   Drabble says that this "Mrs Dalloway-type party" was a deliberate "literary joke" (Cooper-Clark, op. cit., p. 75).

85   Comments to me on 19 June 1984.

86   "Bricks and Mortar," a review of *Arnold Bennett: A Biography*, in *Ms.*, 3 (August 1974), p. 35.

87   "Our Chronicler of Britain," *New York Times Book Review*, 7 September 1980, p. 1.

88   Higdon, interview, op. cit.

BIBLIOGRAPHY

WORKS BY MARGARET DRABBLE

This bibliography lists only first British and American editions of volumes written or edited by Margaret Drabble, her short stories, plays, and non-fiction.

Novels

A Summer Bird-Cage. London: Weidenfeld & Nicolson, 1963. New York: Morrow, 1964.

The Garrick Year. London: Weidenfeld & Nicolson, 1964. New York: Morrow, 1965.

The Millstone. London: Weidenfeld & Nicolson, 1965. New York: Morrow, 1966. *Thank You All Very Much*. New York: New American Library, 1969.

Jerusalem the Golden. London: Weidenfeld & Nicolson, 1967. New York: Morrow, 1967.

The Waterfall. London: Weidenfeld & Nicolson, 1969. New York: Knopf, 1969.

The Needle's Eye. London: Weidenfeld & Nicolson, 1972. New York: Knopf, 1972.

The Realms of Gold. London: Weidenfeld & Nicolson, 1975. New York: Knopf, 1975.

The Ice Age. London: Weidenfeld & Nicolson, 1977. New York: Knopf, 1977.

The Middle Ground. London: Weidenfeld & Nicolson, 1980. New York: Knopf, 1980.

Short stories

"Les Liaisons Dangereuses." *Punch*, 247 (28 October 1964), pp. 646–8.

"Hassan's Tower." In A. D. Maclean (ed.), *Winter's Tales 12*. London: Macmillan, 1966.

"The Reunion." In Kevin Crossley-Holland (ed.), *Winter's Tales 14*. London: Macmillan, 1968.

"A Voyage to Cythera." *Mademoiselle*, 66 (December 1967), pp. 98–9, 148–50.

"Faithful Lovers." *Saturday Evening Post*, 241 (6 April 1968), pp. 62, 64–5.

"A Pyrrhic Victory." *Nova* (July 1968), pp. 80, 84, 86.

"Crossing the Alps." *Penguin Modern Stories 3*. Harmondsworth: Penguin, 1969. Repr. in *Mademoiselle* (February 1971), pp. 154–5, 193–8.

"The Gifts of War." In A. D. Maclean (ed.), *Winter's Tales 16*. London: Macmillan, 1970. Repr. in Susan Cahill (ed.), *Women and Fiction: Short Stories By and About Women*, pp. 335–47. New York: New American Library, 1975.

"A Day in the Life of a Smiling Woman." *Cosmopolitan* (October 1973), pp. 224, 252–7. Repr. in Nancy Dean and Myra Stark (eds), *In the Looking Glass: Twenty-One Modern Short Stories by Women*, pp. 143–65. New York: Putnam, 1977.

"A Success Story." *Spare Rib* (1973). *Ms.* (December 1974), pp. 52–5, 94. Repr. in Ruth Sullivan (ed.), *Fine Lines: The Best of Ms. Fiction*, pp. 259–71. New York: Scribner's, 1982.

"Homework." *Ontario Review*, 7 (1977–8), pp. 7–13.

Plays

Laura. Produced by Granada television, 1964.
Bird of Paradise. Produced in London, 1969.
Isadora (with Melvyn Bragg and Clive Exton). Screenplay, 1969.
A Touch of Love. Screenplay, 1969.

Non-fiction and edited texts

Wordsworth. London: Evans, 1966. New York: Arco, 1969.
London Consequences (Group novel; ed. with B. S. Johnson and contributor). London: Greater London Arts Association, 1972.
Virginia Woolf: A Personal Debt. n.p.: Aloe Editions, 1973.
Arnold Bennett: A Biography. London: Weidenfeld & Nicolson, 1974. New York: Knopf, 1974.
Lady Susan; The Watsons; and Sanditon by Jane Austen (ed.). Harmondsworth: Penguin, 1974.
The Genius of Thomas Hardy (ed.). London: Weidenfeld & Nicolson, 1976. New York: Knopf, 1976.

New Stories 1 (ed. with Charles Osborne). London: Arts Council of Great Britain, 1976.

For Queen and Country: Britain in the Victorian Age (juvenile). London: Deutsch, 1978; New York: Seabury Press, 1979.

A Writer's Britain: Landscape in Literature. London: Thames & Hudson, 1979. New York: Knopf, 1979.

The Tradition of Women's Fiction: Lectures in Japan (ed. Yukako Suga). Tokyo: Oxford University Press, 1982.

Oxford Companion to English Literature, 5th edn (ed.). London: Oxford University Press, forthcoming.

Selected articles

"Baffled! Margaret Drabble stalks uncomprehendingly round the mystery of masculinity." *Punch*, 24 July 1968, pp. 122–4.

"Women Novelists." *Books*, 375 (1968), pp. 87–90.

"Letter to the Editor." *The Times Literary Supplement*, 5 June 1969, p. 612 (about the value of an education for a creative writer).

"Money as a Subject for the Novelist." *The Times Literary Supplement*, 24 July 1969, pp. 792–3.

"Doris Lessing: Cassandra in a World Under Siege." *Ramparts*, 10, 8 (February 1972), pp. 50–4.

"Margaret Drabble on Virginia Woolf." *Harpers Bazaar and Queen* (September 1972), pp. 90–1. Shortened as "How Not to be Afraid of Virginia Woolf." *Ms.* (November 1972), pp. 68–70, 72, 121.

"A Woman Writer." *Books*, 11 (Spring 1973), 4–6. Repr. in Michelene Wandor (ed.), *On Gender and Writing*, pp. 156–9. London and Boston: Pandora Press, 1983.

"The War between Women and Women." *The Times*, 23 July 1973, p. 9.

"The Writer as Recluse: The Theme of Solitude in the Works of the Brontës." *Brontë Society Transactions*, 16 (1974), pp. 259–69.

"The Author Comments" on Monica Lauritzen Mannheimer, "The Search for Identity in Margaret Drabble's *The Needle's Eye*." *Dutch Quarterly Review of Anglo-American Letters*, 5, 1 (1975), pp. 35–8.

"A Book I Love: Margaret Drabble on the Novels of Angus Wilson." *Mademoiselle* (August 1975), pp. 94, 106.

"Introduction" to Emily Brontë, *Wuthering Heights* (ed. P. Henderson), pp. v–xxii. London: J. M. Dent & Sons, 1978.

"Are the social graces suspect? Is art itself suspect?" *The Listener*, 10 (July 1980), pp. 51–2.

"'No Idle Rentier': Angus Wilson and the Nourished Literary

Imagination." *Studies in the Literary Imagination*, 13 (Spring 1980), pp. 119–29.

"Gone but Not Quite Forgotten." *New York Times Book Review*, 25 July 1982, pp. 6, 25.

"Introduction" to Frieda Lawrence, *Not I But the Wind*, pp. vi–xii. London: Granada, 1983.

"J. G. Farrell." In Susan Hill (ed.), *People: Essays and Poems*, pp. 43–8. London: Hogarth Press, 1983.

"Novelists as Inspired Gossips." *Ms.* (April 1983), pp. 32, 34.

Selected interviews

Clare, John. "Margaret Drabble's Everyday Hell." *The Times*, 27 March 1972, p. 6.

Cooper-Clark, Diana. "Margaret Drabble: Cautious Feminist." *Atlantic Monthly*, 246 (November 1980), pp. 69–75.

Creighton, Joanne V. "An Interview with Margaret Drabble." In Dorey Schmidt (ed.), *Margaret Drabble: Golden Realms*, pp. 18–31. Edinburg, Texas: Pan American University Press, 1980.

Firchow, Peter. "Margaret Drabble." *The Writer's Place: Interviews on the Literary Situation in Contemporary Britain*, pp. 102–21. Minneapolis: University of Minnesota Press, 1974.

Hardin, Nancy S. "An Interview with Margaret Drabble." *Contemporary Literature*, 14, 3 (Summer 1973), pp. 273–95.

Milton, Barbara. "Margaret Drabble: The Art of Fiction LXX." *Paris Review*, 20 (Fall–Winter 1978), pp. 40–65.

Parker, Gillian, and Todd, Janet. "Margaret Drabble." In Janet Todd (ed.), *Women Writers Talking*, pp. 160–78. New York: Holmes & Meier, 1983.

Poland, Nancy. "Margaret Drabble: 'There Must Be a Lot of People Like Me.'" *Midwest Quarterly*, 16, 3 (Spring 1975), pp. 255–67.

Preussner, Dee. "Talking with Margaret Drabble." *Modern Fiction Studies*, 25 (Winter 1979/80), pp. 563–77.

Rozencwajg, Iris. "Interview with Margaret Drabble." *Women's Studies*, 6 (1979), pp. 335–47.

BIBLIOGRAPHY

Korenman, Joan S. "A Margaret Drabble Bibliography." In Ellen Cronan Rose (ed.), *Critical Essays on Margaret Drabble*. Boston, Mass.: G. K. Hall, 1985.

SELECTED CRITICISM OF MARGARET DRABBLE

Books

Moran, Mary Hurley. *Margaret Drabble: Existing Within Structures.* Carbondale, Ill.: Southern Illinois University Press, 1983.

Myer, Valerie Grosvenor. *Margaret Drabble: Puritanism and Permissiveness.* London: Vision Press, 1974. New York: Harper, 1974.

Rose, Ellen Cronan. *The Novels of Margaret Drabble: Equivocal Figures.* London: Macmillan, 1980. Totowa, NJ: Barnes & Noble, 1980.

—— (ed.). *Critical Essays on Margaret Drabble.* Boston, Mass.: G. K. Hall, 1985.

Schmidt, Dorey (ed.). *Margaret Drabble: Golden Realms.* Edinburg, Texas: Pan American University Press, 1980.

Articles

This listing is highly selective. See Korenman's bibliography for an extensive list of critical works on Drabble.

Beards, Virginia K. "Margaret Drabble: Novels of a Cautious Feminist." *Critique,* 15, 1 (1973), pp. 35–47.

Bergonzi, Bernard. "Drabble, Margaret." In James Vinson (ed.), *Contemporary Novelists,* 3rd edn, pp. 184–5. New York: St Martin's, 1982.

Butler, Colin. "Margaret Drabble: *The Millstone* and Wordsworth." *English Studies,* 59 (1978), pp. 353–60.

Campbell, Jane. "Margaret Drabble and the Search for Analogy." In Jane Campbell and James Doyle (eds), *The Practical Vision: Essays in English Literature in Honour of Flora Roy,* pp. 133–50. Waterloo, Ontario: Wilfrid Laurier University Press, 1978.

Creighton, Joanne V. "The Reader and Modern and Post Modern Fiction." *College Literature,* 9 (Fall 1982), pp. 216–30.

—— "Reading Margaret Drabble's *The Waterfall.*" In Ellen Cronan Rose (ed.), *Critical Essays on Margaret Drabble.* Boston: G. K. Hall, 1985.

Davis, Cynthia A. "Unfolding Form: Narrative Approach and Theme in *The Realms of Gold.*" *Modern Language Quarterly,* 40 (December 1979), pp. 390–402.

Firchow, Peter E. "Rosamund's Complaint: Margaret Drabble's *The Millstone.*" In Robert K. Morris (ed.), *Old Lines, New Forces: Essays on the Contemporary British Novel, 1969–1970.* Madison, NJ: Fairleigh Dickinson University Press, 1976. London: Associated University Presses, 1976.

Fox-Genovese, Elizabeth. "The Ambiguities of Female Identity: A Reading of the Novels of Margaret Drabble." *Partisan Review*, 46 (1979), pp. 234–48.

Gindin, James. "Three Recent British Novels and an American Response." *Michigan Quarterly Review*, 17 (1978), pp. 223–46.

Harper, Michael F. "Margaret Drabble and the Resurrection of the English Novel." *Contemporary Literature*, 23, 2 (1982), pp. 145–68.

Higdon, David Leon. "'Its Lines Were the Lines of Memory': Margaret Drabble, *The Realms of Gold*". In *Shadows of the Past in Contemporary British Fiction*. London: Macmillan, 1985.

Joseph, Gerhard. "Antigone as Cultural Touchstone: Matthew Arnold, George Eliot, Virginia Woolf, and Margaret Drabble." *PMLA*, 96 (January 1981), pp. 22–35.

Korenman, Joan S. "The Liberation of Margaret Drabble." *Critique*, 21 (Fall 1980), pp. 61–72.

Lambert, Ellen Z. "Margaret Drabble and the Sense of Possibility." *University of Toronto Quarterly*, 49 (Spring 1980), pp. 228–51.

Lay, Mary M. "Temporal Ordering in the Fiction of Margaret Drabble." *Critique*, 21(Fall 1980), pp. 73–84.

Levitt, Morton P. "The New Victorians: Margaret Drabble as Trollope." In Dorey Schmidt (ed.), *Margaret Drabble: Golden Realms*, pp. 168–77. Edinburg, Texas: Pan American University Press, 1980.

Libby, Marion Vlastos. "Fate and Feminism in the Novels of Margaret Drabble." *Contemporary Literature*, 16 (Spring 1975), pp. 175–92.

MacCarthy, Fiona. "The Drabble Sisters." *The Guardian*, 13 April 1967, p. 8.

Manheimer, Joan. "Margaret Drabble and the Journey to the Self." *Studies in the Literary Imagination*, 11 (Fall 1978), pp. 127–43.

Mannheimer, Monica Lauritzen. "The Search for Identity in Margaret Drabble's *The Needle's Eye*." *Dutch Quarterly Review for Anglo-American Letters*, 5, 1 (1975), pp. 24–35.

Rose, Ellen Cronan. "Margaret Drabble: Surviving the Future." *Critique*, 15, 1 (1973), pp. 5–21.

—— "Feminine Endings – and Beginnings: Margaret Drabble's *The Waterfall*." *Contemporary Literature*, 21 (Winter 1980), pp. 81–99.

—— "Drabble's *The Middle Ground*: 'Mid-Life' Narrative Strategies." *Critique*, 23, 3 (1982), pp. 69–82.

Sage, Lorna. "Female Fictions: The Women Novelists." In Malcolm Bradbury and David Palmer (eds), *The Contemporary English*

Novel, pp. 66–87. London: Edward Arnold, 1979. New York: Holmes & Meier, 1980.

Spitzer, Susan. "Fantasy and Femaleness in Margaret Drabble's *The Millstone*." *Novel*, 11 (Spring 1978), pp. 227–45.

Stovel, Nora F. "Margaret Drabble's Golden Vision." In Ellen Cronan Rose (ed.), *Margaret Drabble: Golden Realms*, pp. 3–17. Edinburg, Texas: Pan American University Press, 1980.

Whittier, Gayle. "Mistresses and Madonnas in the Novels of Margaret Drabble." *Women and Literature*, 1 (1980), pp. 197–313.

Williams, Pat. "The Sisters Drabble." *Sunday Times Magazine*, 6 August 1967, pp. 12–15.

Wilson, Keith. "Jim, Jake and the Years Between: The Will to Stasis in the Contemporary British Novel." *Ariel: A Review of International English Literature*, 13 (January 1982), pp. 55–69.